Shoulder injuries in sports

Shoulder injuries in sports

Phillip J Marone, MD

Director, Division of Sports Medicine
Department of Orthopaedics
Thomas Jefferson University Hospital

Chairman, Department of Orthopaedic Surgery
Physical Medicine and Rehabilitation
Methodist Hospital

Philadelphia
Pennsylvania
USA

Martin Dunitz

First published in the United Kingdom by
Martin Dunitz Ltd, The Livery House, 7–9 Pratt Street,
London NW1 0AE

A CIP catalogue record for this book is available from the British Library.

ISBN 1–85317–095–X

Composition by TecSet Ltd, Wallington, Surrey
Printed and bound in Great Britain by
The University Press, Cambridge

Contents

Foreword

The opening chapters of *Shoulder injuries in sports*, presented clearly and succinctly, deal with the most recent concepts of the functional anatomy and the biomechanics of the shoulder; concepts that are so essential in understanding the mechanisms of injuries in the throwing arm, and that always play a significant role in the diagnosis and management of these injuries.

The chapter on investigative techniques is masterfully presented. It describes not only the routine techniques in radiography of the shoulder, but puts emphasis on the importance of MRI and arthroscopic examinations to show lesions of the soft tissues and osseous elements of all components of the shoulder joint.

The subsequent chapters, dealing with the mechanisms, diagnosis, and management of injuries of the shoulder region (sternoclavicular joint, acromioclavicular joint, glenohumeral joint, and scapulothoracic articula-

tion), are of great importance to all those treating shoulder injuries, be these produced in sport or industry, or accidentally.

The chapter on rehabilitation of the upper extremity is invaluable to all concerned with restoration of normal function after shoulder injuries. The methods are clearly demonstrated in detail, and represent the experience of years in dealing with injuries of the shoulder.

This book is a 'must' in the library of all physicians at all levels—from the intern to the accomplished orthopaedic surgeon. It presents the most modern concepts in mechanisms, diagnosis, and management of shoulder injuries in sport, all of which reflect the long years of experience and dedication of the author to the art and science of a particular field and the ability to share this knowledge with others.

Anthony F. DePalma

Acknowledgments

When one authors a book, it is important to realize that even though one is the sole contributor to the factual material in the book, there are many who have played an integral part in its creation.

Ms Mary Banks, Publishing Director of Martin Dunitz Ltd, contacted me at the suggestion of Joseph Torg, MD, regarding the creation of a book about the shoulder problems in sport-active individuals. Joseph Torg deserves credit for his belief in my ability to author this book; Ms Banks, who gave much guidance for the project, was very helpful.

The research material was gathered, and during that period there were a number of individuals who helped, especially Donald Seger and the orthopaedic residents at Jefferson.

The collection of the photographs was an enormous chore. I have to thank the residents at Jefferson, some of whom are depicted in this book, some of the Philadelphia Phillies baseball players, and the trainers of the Phillies. Rod Hampton and Susan Lyne, who produced the photographs, accommodated all my requests and did so in an exemplary fashion. The following figures are reproduced by courtesy of the Department of Radiology, Thomas Jefferson University Hospital, Philadelphia, Pennsylvania: 5.2, 5.4, 5.6, 5.8, 5.10, 5.14–5.21, 6.2, 6.4, 6.6, 6.9, 6.14, 7.1–7.3, 9.3–9.5, 10.4, 10.5, 10.12, 11.1–11.4, 11.7, 12.3, 13.2. The following figures are reproduced by courtesy of Lawrence S. Miller, MD: 5.22–5.24, 11.6.

The manuscript had to be revised so often that my secretary, Cheryl Vanartsdalen-Tatum, has come to know this book as well as I. To Cheryl I say thank you for your patience, your help, and your thoughtfulness throughout this process.

My thanks are due to Donald Seger, my friend and co-worker, who collated the photographic material, put the references in their proper order, and reviewed the manuscript with me.

To my immediate family I say thanks for your constant encouragement and understanding throughout this process.

My mentor and friend, Anthony DePalma, MD, I thank for his role in my career, as it was during my period of training with Dr DePalma that I learned what hard work and perseverance would enable one to accomplish. I also thank Dr DePalma for reviewing the book and writing its Foreword.

To all the people I have treated with shoulder injuries, especially those involved in throwing sports, I extend my thanks since they gave me the privilage of becoming an expert in this field.

To Martin Dunitz, Stuart McRobbie, Publisher, Alison Campbell, Managing Editor, and Robert Peden, the Editor, I offer my deepest gratitude for their constant help with the book. The British reviewers of the manuscript I thank for their constructive criticism. Their review of the manuscript was important to me and played a large role in the final production.

Much thought was given to the structure of the book: as you will see, the book begins with anatomy, followed by biomechanics, then proceeds in a systematic regional fashion, enabling the reader to obtain the most useful knowledge of problems of the shoulder in sports. At times a section may seem redundant; however, this approach was deliberate, in an effort to reinforce pertinent information in the mind of the reader.

1
Functional anatomy

Muscles act to create motion, restrain passive motion, or maintain a stationary posture, and in these capacities, they serve as accelerators, decelerators, and stabilizers, respectively. Postural stability, selective motion, and dynamic stability are the three demands necessary to control muscle action. Certain sporting activities commonly involved with shoulder function are described in Table 1.1.

The forequarter is suspended from the body through the clavicle at the sternum. The glenohumeral and scapulothoracic musculature must meet the demands listed above in order to maintain forequarter stability since the only bony attachment of the upper extremity to the sternum is the clavicle. Optimal function depends upon appropriate muscle strength, muscle tone, and synchronous motion.

Musculature controlling the glenohumeral joint

The deltoid, clavicular portion of the pectoralis major, and coracobrachialis function primarily as elevators of the arm. The rotator cuff musculature, characterized by short

Table 1.1

Sporting activities commonly involved with shoulder function.

Throwing Sports
        Baseball
        Football
Racquet Sports
        Tennis
        Racquet ball
        Squash
Swimming
Weightlifting
Wrestling
Others
        Basketball
        Diving
        Dance
        Gymnastics
        Golf
        Ice hockey
        Martial arts
        Shooting
        Snow skiing

 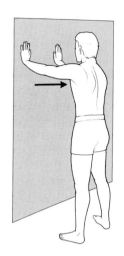

Figure 1.1

The peripheral musculature attached to the humerus reacts to move the body away from an object.

Figure 1.2

The arm swinging, as in walking or running, produces an intense pattern of muscle action of the supraspinatus and posterior deltoid.

muscle fibers that maintain close proximity of the joint, has two functions, notably rotation and joint stabilization. The setting of the humerus by this musculature aids in the normal glenohumeral rhythm that is necessary for the painless synchronous act of shoulder motion. The peripheral muscles attached to the humerus are the latissimus dorsi, teres major, and the sternal head of the pectoralis major, all of which provide rapid descent of the arm (Table 1.2). The same group of muscles are also means of raising the trunk with the arms, that is, moving the body away from an object (*Figure 1.1*).

Postural stability

In the relaxed erect position, none of the musculature about the shoulder joint has been found to display electromyogram (EMG) activity. If there is downward pressure on the arm, such as a weight in the hand, there is a strong response in the supraspinatus and a weak reaction in the posterior deltoid with no activity identified in the middle deltoid or biceps. When the arm is swinging, such as in walking or running (*Figure 1.2*), there is a similar but more intense pattern of muscle action (*Figure 1.3*). Continuous supraspinatus activity,

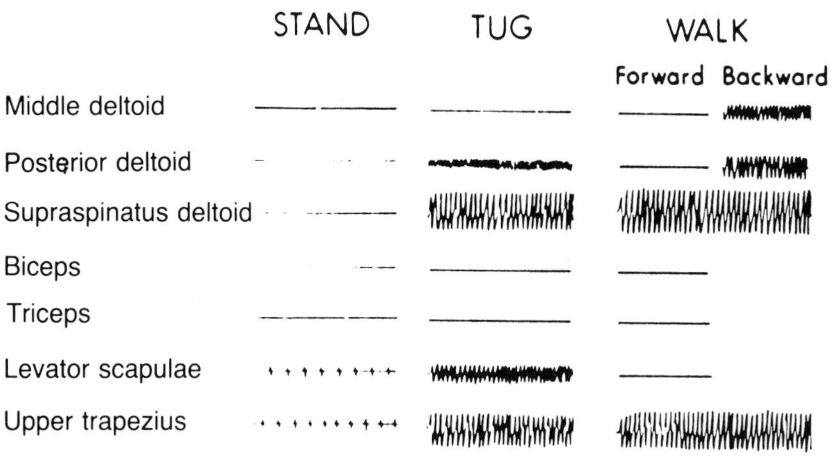

	STAND	TUG	WALK		Figure 1.3
			Forward	Backward	EMG activity when the
Middle deltoid	—— —	—— —	—— —	ᴧᴧᴧᴧᴧ	arms are swinging (courtesy of Rowe 1988, p. 19).
Posterior deltoid	- ... -	ᴧᴧᴧᴧᴧᴧ	—— —	ᴧᴧᴧᴧᴧᴧ	
Supraspinatus deltoid	· ---- —	ᴧᴧᴧᴧᴧᴧᴧᴧ	ᴧᴧᴧᴧᴧᴧᴧᴧᴧᴧ		
Biceps		— —	—— —	——	
Triceps	—— ——	—— —	——		
Levator scapulae	⸰ ⸰ ⸰ ⸰ ⸰⸰⸰	ᴧᴧᴧᴧᴧᴧᴧ	——		
Upper trapezius	⸰ ⸰ ⸰ ⸰ ⸰⸰⸰ ⸰↔	ᴧᴧᴧᴧᴧᴧᴧᴧ	ᴧᴧᴧᴧᴧᴧᴧᴧᴧ		

Table 1.2

Musculature controlling the glenohumeral joint.

Deltoid
Pectoralis major
Coracobrachialis
Biceps brachii
Supraspinatus
Subscapularis
Infraspinatus
Teres minor
Teres major
Latissimus dorsi

coupled with posterior and middle deltoid activity, occurs during the period of arm extension and at the termination of flexion. Deceleration of flexion is assisted by the latissimus dorsi and teres major.

Dynamic stability

The rotator cuff is the key to dynamic glenohumeral stability, since it functions to reduce the shearing strain experienced by the joint. This reduction in strain is accomplished by fiber alignment and the immediate proximity of the insertion sites to the joint margin. Both compressive and shear forces are created to stabilize the humeral head on the glenoid (*Figure 1.4*). Alignment of the deltoid induces a significant shear force as the muscle elevates the arm, with the greatest pressure at 90° of abduction, while synchronous action by the rotator cuff provides protective counterforces.

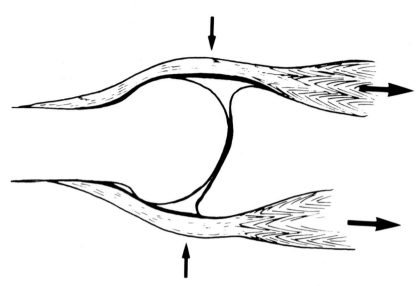

Figure 1.4

Compressive and encircling shear forces are created by the rotator cuff musculature to stabilize the humeral head on the glenoid fossa (courtesy of Rowe 1988, p. 20).

Shoulder motion

The action of raising the arm from the neutral position is a basic shoulder motion. This is a very versatile act since the hand can be placed anywhere in space from 0–180° of total motion. This control is very selective and precise. In order to raise the arm, the deltoid and underlying supraspinatus must act in synergy, as they create the dominant forces.

The deltoid functions as three distinct muscles through its anterior, middle, and posterior portions. The middle deltoid, the largest portion, is dominant and participates in all arm activities. Supplementing this action are the anterior and posterior deltoids, since they act synergistically to adductor and abductor forces or assume primary responsibility for flexion and extension. Flexion is accomplished mainly by the anterior deltoid, and is assisted by the clavicular head of the pectoralis major, the coracobrachialis, and the biceps brachii. Extension of the arm is dominated by the posterior deltoid, with strong participation from the middle deltoid; the anterior deltoid, however, remains silent. The deltoid fibers shorten as they travel from the dependent rest position to full glenohumeral elevation. Anatomically, this represents a significant (33 percent) reduction in the length of the muscle (*Figure 1.5*). If the scapula is held rigidly to the chest wall, the arm can be raised actively to 90°. This position of 90° is insufficient to accept any additional resistance, therefore the loss of deltoid strength is avoided by scapular rotation. This synergistic action not only preserves the deltoid force, but reduces its demand by placing the glenoid under the humeral head for added support (*Figure 1.6*). **Deltoid function is dependent upon scapulohumeral rhythm.**

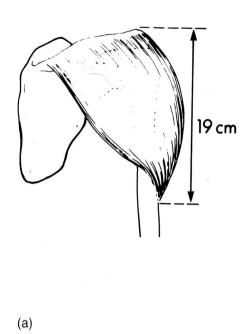

(a)

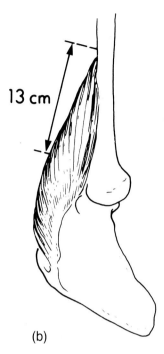

(b)

Figure 1.5

The deltoid muscle length is reduced between (a) the resting position and (b) full arm elevation (courtesy of Rowe 1988, p. 22).

The supraspinatus muscle

This muscle was considered in the past to be inadequate in initiating and maintaining forward flexion in the scapular plane. The rationale was that its short leverage and modest size would limit the torque that can be produced. This has been demonstrated to be inaccurate since the torque produced by the supraspinatus is equal to the torque of the deltoid in forward flexion in the scapular plane. Dynamic EMG results revealed that the middle and anterior deltoid functioned equally with the supraspinatus. Through their combined action, the calculated intensity of each muscle is 50 percent of the maximum strength of each muscle.

The remaining rotator cuff musculature contributes to the force couple that facilitates arm elevation, but does not have any direct effect on forward flexion in the scapular plane. Studies of nerve block have demonstrated that the synergistic action between the deltoid and supraspinatus musculature is not essential for full arm elevation. Approximately 50 percent of normal strength is lost when either muscle has been blocked through its respective nerves. Since the remaining muscles — infraspinatus, teres minor, and subscapularis — have different innervations than the deltoid and supraspinatus, it seems clear that those muscles actively provide a minimal counterforce to preserve alignment of the humeral head. If simultaneous blocking

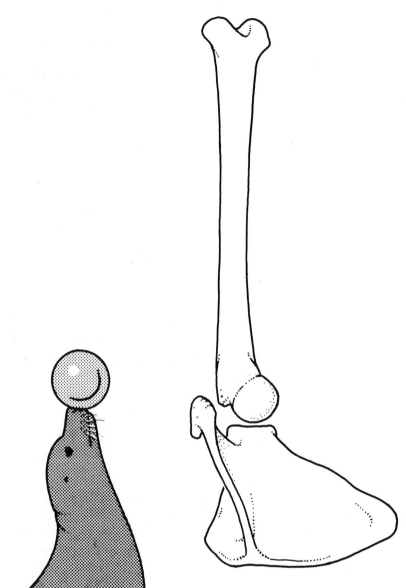

Figure 1.6

The glenoid fossa functions like the nose of a seal while balancing a ball (after Rowe 1988, p. xx).

of the axillary and suprascapular nerves occurs, there is inability to raise the arm from its dependent position.

The infraspinatus muscle

The activity of the infraspinatus muscle is questionable as to its effect in arm elevation. Electromyographically, the infraspinatus is the next most active rotator muscle after the supraspinatus. It does have a potential contribution to glenohumeral joint stability, therefore enhancing its participation in arm elevation. The prime function of the infraspinatus is external humeral rotation on the glenoid.

The subscapularis muscle

The subscapularis plays an important role in glenohumeral stability, enhancing arm elevation. It is a humeral rotator on the glenoid in internal rotation and functions in concert with the other internal rotators of the shoulder, namely the pectoralis major, teres major, and latissimus dorsi.

The biceps brachii muscle

The biceps brachii muscle is a humeral head depressor. It has been shown to play a very small role in elevation and rotation of the shoulder.

Musculature about the scapulothoracic area

Upward rotation of the arm in conjunction with arm elevation and postural support of the scapula is the function of four scapulothoracic muscles — the trapezius, rhomboids, levator scapulae, and serratus anterior — directly controlling the scapula. As one sits or stands, the weight of the arm tends to draw the scapula downward (*Figure 1.7*). Passive scapular suspension is available from the deep fascia of the neck as it extends from the head to the clavicle and spine of the scapula, enclosing the trapezius and sternocleidomastoid muscles. Active suspension is modified by the levator scapula and upper trapezius, with the levator scapula being the larger of the two muscles (*Figure 1.8*). **If a load is added to the hand or there is active elevation of the scapula, a brisk response by the levator and upper trapezius is elicited.**

Rotation of the scapula is important for synchronous arm elevation. The trapezius and serratus muscles, recognized as the upper rotators of the scapula, act together to accomplish scapular rotation (*Figure 1.9*). Inman et al (1944) identified a force couple in each muscle composed of upper and lower segments, which produced upward rotation of the scapula (*Figures 1.9, 1.10*). Upward rotation of the scapula can also be produced by the upper transverse fibers of the serratus. This rotation serves three functions: (1) it provides a stabilizing base for the humerus by moving the glenoid underneath the arm as it is raised; (2) the deltoid fiber length is preserved as the acromial/humeral distance is maintained; and (3) upward rotation of the acromial arch also lessens the potential for humeral impingement at the end of arm range. **In order to attain maximum scapular rotation, the trapezius and serratus must be effective.**

The ability to draw the scapula back towards the midline accentuates horizontal extension of the arm and is known as scapular

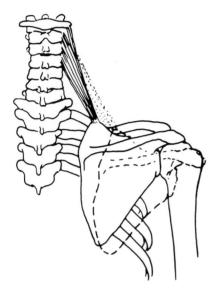

Figure 1.7

Levator scapulae tension is reduced by the
passive forward droop of the scapula (courtesy of
Rowe 1988, p. 29).

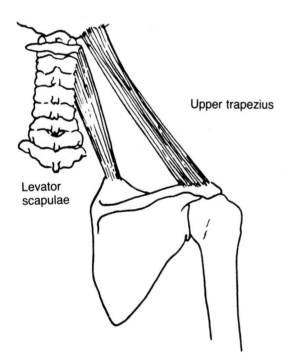

Figure 1.8

Active suspension of the scapula with the arm
dependent (courtesy of Rowe 1988, p. 29).

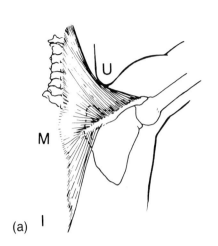

(a)

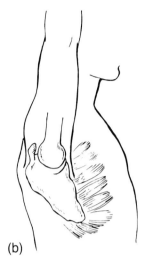

(b)

Figure 1.9

Dominant rotators of the scapula during arm elevation. (a) Trapezius: U, upper; M, middle; I, inferior; (b) serratus anterior. (Courtesy of Rowe 1988, p. 30.)

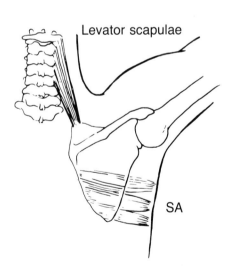

Figure 1.10

Serratus force couple. Upper force = levator scapulae; lower force = digits 5 and 6 of serratus anterior (SA). (Courtesy of Rowe 1988, p. 31.)

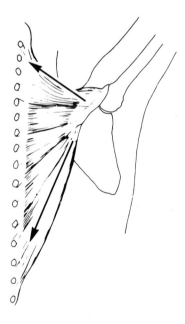

Figure 1.11

Trapezius force couple. Upper force = upper trapezius; lower force = lower trapezius. (Courtesy of Rowe 1988, p. 31.)

adduction. Indirect muscle control is provided by the middle trapezius and rhomboids. The latissimus dorsi also retracts the scapula. The scapula advancing anteriorly on the thorax is referred to as 'protraction'; protraction is the function of the serratus anterior. The follow-through motion that occurs in throwing sports, tennis, and swimming includes scapular protraction.

2
Biomechanics of the shoulder

The shoulder is a complex organ that suspends the arm and provides a base from which the upper extremity functions as a prehensile organ in total global motion. Its intrinsic mechanism permits the upper extremity to lift heavy loads below the horizontal plane and to support such loads above the plane. The shoulder, accompanied by movements of the lower extremity, the pelvis, and the trunk, allows the arm to propel objects with great speed and power. From a functional viewpoint, the shoulder comprises three synovial joints (the sternoclavicular, the acromioclavicular, and the glenohumeral) and two articulations (the scapulothoracic and the coracoacromial) (*Figure 2.1*).

Bony suspension of the shoulder girdle and arm is by the clavicle since it is the single structure that suspends the scapula and the arm from the axial skeleton. The medial end of the clavicle articulates with the sternum, establishing the only synovial joint between the upper extremity and the axial skeleton.

Suspension of the shoulder from the clavicle functions through a strong system of suspensory muscles comprising the trapezius, sternomastoid, and the levator musculature (*Figure 2.2*).

The trapezius muscle, composed of three distinct parts, functions as a single unit since it supports and holds the shoulder backwards. The upper segment elevates the shoulder as in a shrugging motion and, together with the middle fibers, it pulls the scapula upward and inward. The lower fibers participate in elevation of the arm by steadying the scapula against the thoracic cage. **The trapezius plays a major role in rotation of the scapula about the chest during circumduction of the arm.**

The role of the rotator cuff

The glenohumeral joint lacks bony stability and relies on its capsular tissue, glenoid labrum, ligaments, and musculature about the shoulder joint for its stability. A small area of contact exists between the humerus and glenoid during elevation of the arm. Additional stability is aided by the humerus setting in the glenoid fossa by the action of the supraspinatus and by the ability of the scapula to rotate so that, regardless of the position of the arm, the glenoid fossa is always in a position of stability in order to support the head of the humerus in its orderly motions.

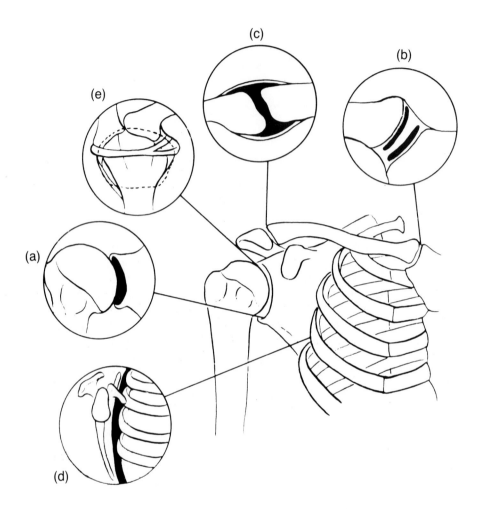

Figure 2.1

The shoulder comprises three synovial joints: (a)
the glenohumeral, (b) the sternoclavicular, and (c)
the acromioclavicular. The articulations are (d)
the scapulothoracic and (e) the subcoroacromial.
(Courtesy of DePalma 1983, p. 66).

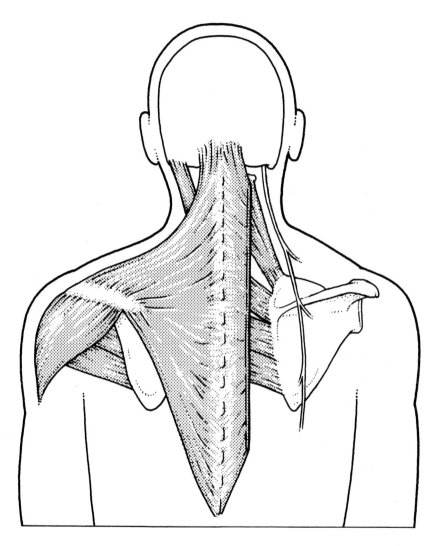

Figure 2.2

The trapezius, levator scapulae, and sternomastoid serve as suspensory muscles of the shoulder (courtesy of DePalma 1983, p. 66).

The capsular role

Superior, anterior, and posterior capsules blend with the tendinous insertion of the rotator muscles. Together with the coraco-humeral ligament these provide stability of the glenohumeral joint (*Figure 2.3*).

The role of the deltoid

The deltoid is the most important structure involved with supporting the arm below the level of the clavicle. Its origin drapes the entire shoulder girdle, thus permitting the deltoid to participate in all movements of

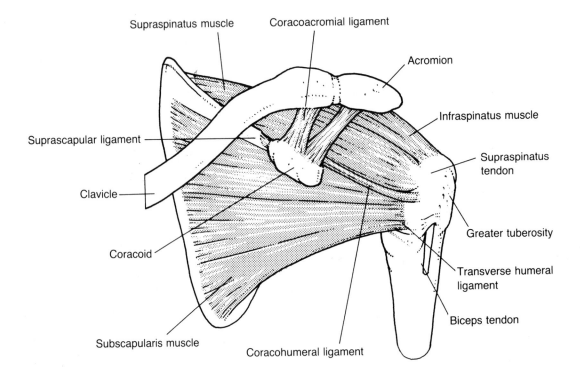

Figure 2.3

The stability of the glenohumeral joint is provided by the superior, anterior, and posterior capsule blending with the tendinous insertion of the rotator muscles acting together with the coracohumeral ligament (courtesy of DePalma 1983, p. 67).

the arm. These movements are performed in concert with the normal rotation of the scapula.

Prevention of downward displacement of the arm

Under normal conditions, the scapula assumes an upward, lateral and forward position so that the glenoid fossa lies in an oblique plane. When the head of the humerus tends to migrate downwards, it is forced laterally. The superior portion of the capsule, the supraspinatus, and the posterior deltoid, are so oriented that they resist lateral migration of the head of the humerus and hence prevent its downward displacement, as shown by Basmajian and Bazant (1959) (*Figure 2.4*). It appears that under ordinary conditions with the arm unloaded, the pull of gravity is resisted by the

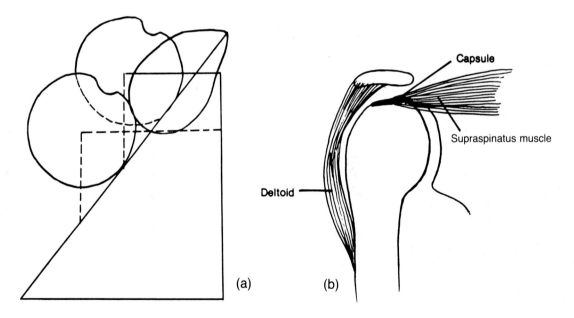

Figure 2.4

(a) In downward displacement, the humeral head is also displaced laterally. (b) This is resisted by the orientation of the capsule, supraspinatus, and posterior deltoid whose fibers run horizontally. (Courtesy of DePalma 1983, p. 70.)

superior capsule and coracohumeral ligament.

Scapular motion

Of all the bony elements comprising the
shoulder joint, the scapula is one that is
ingeniously devised. It is able to shift in all
directions since it lies on the posterior chest
wall in a multilayered muscular bed. The
ample anterior and posterior fossae provide
large surface areas for the origin of the rotator
muscles that control the movements of the
head of the humerus. The glenoid fossa is
tilted upward and anteriorly so that it affords
a base for the humeral head regardless of the
position of the arm in relation to the trunk.
Through its intrinsic muscular mechanism,
the scapula functions as a stable, yet movable,
base for the upper extremity. **Disorders that
disrupt the stability and orderly movements
of the scapula will also disrupt the movements of the arm**.

3

The shoulder in throwing sports

In an effort to understand how to prevent and treat overuse injuries secondary to a throwing motion it is important to understand this action. **The use of a correct throwing motion with proper body mechanics is very important in the prevention of overuse injuries to the shoulder.**

Every athlete involved in throwing sports should have a preparticipation examination. By this means, one can find evidence of muscular weakness, asynchronous motion, lost motion, and pain. The upper extremity accounts for 75 percent of injuries in throwing sports, with the shoulder being the most common anatomical structure of the upper extremity involved. Rotator cuff lesions (including impingement syndrome and tears), subluxation (anterior–posterior and inferior), glenoid–labral tears, acromioclavicular joint injuries, muscle strains, proximal humeral physeal separations, vascular injuries, effort thrombosis, and nerve entrapments are the most common problems encountered in throwing sports.

The pitching mechanism

The pitching mechanism has been studied by many investigators and has been well described. Jobe et al (1983) and McLeod (1985) divided the pitching motion into five phases (*Figure 3.1*).

The wind-up phase

In the wind-up phase, the opposite leg is cocked, and the ball is removed from the glove.

The cocking phase

In the cocking phase, the ipsilateral leg is planted in front of the body while the pelvis rotates internally. The shoulder is abducted 90°, with the humerus maximally rotated ex-

Figure 3.1

(a) The wind-up phase: ball is removed from glove as opposite leg is cocked. (b) The cocking phase: shoulder is abducted 90° with the humerus maximally externally rotated. (c) The acceleration phase: forceful internal rotation of the humerus after forward motion of the chest and shoulder stops. (d) The release/deceleration phase: ball release occurs 8–10 msec, calling up deceleration forces twice as strong as the acceleration forces. (e) Follow-through phase: the body moves forward after release, reducing distraction forces across the shoulder, thereby reducing tension on the rotator cuff.

ternally, placing the anterior shoulder capsule under tension. The deltoid, supraspinatus, infraspinatus, and teres minor muscles undergo forceful contraction and the chest and shoulder advances forward.

The acceleration phase

The acceleration phase begins when the forward movement of the chest and shoulder stops. The body is brought forward and the arm follows behind. The latissimus dorsi, pectoralis major, and teres major muscles contract. Valgus tension stress is applied to the elbow as the arm whips forward. The energy developed by the body moving forward is transferred to the arm to accelerate the humerus. The internal rotators contract forcefully while the external rotators, infraspinatus, and teres minor eccentrically contract forcefully imparting deceleration forces to the horizontal adduction movement of the humerus.

The release and deceleration phase

Decelerating forces are approximately twice as strong as acceleration forces. Ball release occurs over approximately 8–10 ms. At ball release, the arm motion must be quickly decelerated to prevent the humeral head from subluxating posteriorly. The rotator cuff and deltoid muscles must therefore contract. The humerus internally rotates quickly as the elbow is rapidly extending. Considerable forearm pronation results, with high forces being transferred across the elbow to the lateral side, causing compression forces between the radius and capitulum. As the forearm extends fully on the humerus the

olecranon process of the ulna impinges upon the olecranon fossa of the humerus.

The follow-through phase

As the body moves forward with the arm, it reduces distraction forces across the shoulder, thereby reducing tension on the rotator cuff. The opposite leg is planted, helping the pitcher maintain balance during the smooth transition from violent deceleration to recovery.

Adaptive anatomical changes noted in throwing sports

The dominant arm demonstrates hypertrophy of the musculature and bones. External rotation is significantly increased, while there is a marked decrease in internal rotation compared to the nondominant shoulder. If there is a significant difference of external rotation strength as compared to internal rotation muscle strength, this is an indication of rotator cuff injury. If there is a significant decrease in external and internal rotation, this also is an indication of shoulder injury.

Burk et al (1991) in a magnetic resonance imaging (MRI) study found cortical irregularity and/or subchondral cyst formation at the posterior aspect of the greater tuberosity near the insertion site of the infraspinatus tendon in five of seven players with rotator cuff tears. Similar findings were noted in an asymptomatic volunteer and in one of the three players without a cuff tear who also had irregular thickening of the posterior capsule. These findings are believed to represent chronic avulsive changes resulting from the deceleration stresses of the follow-through motion.

Other problems encountered in the throwing act are noted in Table 3.1.

Table 3.1

Problems encountered in the pitching act.

Rotator cuff injury and impingement
syndrome
Anterior glenohumeral subluxation
Posterior glenohumeral subluxation
Glenoid–labral tears
     Anterior
     Posterior
     Superior labrum from anterior to
     posterior (SLAP) lesion
Bennett lesion (ossification of the
posterior–inferior glenoid rim)
Proximal humeral physeal separation
Tendonitis other than rotator cuff
     Pectoralis major
     Latissimus dorsi
     Teres major
     Biccipital tendinitis
Rupture of the latissimus (reported in
baseball by Barnes and Tullos 1978)
Rupture of the pectoralis major muscle
Cortical irregularity and/or subchondral cyst
formation at the posterior aspect of the
greater tuberosity, with irregular thickening
of the posterior capsule

Summation of the throwing act

The mechanism of the throwing act consists of components responsible for positioning the scapula, humerus, and forearm within relatively narrow tolerances, thereby controlling total arm advancement. The deltoid musculature provides shoulder elevation, with the rotator cuff being responsible for the adjustment and fine tuning of the position. The capsule is wound up prior to the forward propulsion of the arm and ball. The serratus anterior functions to maintain the scapula against the chest wall, thereby providing a stable glenoid platform. The latissimus dorsi and pectoralis major contribute power and driving force to the acceleration and follow-through phase. The triceps and biceps work in concert with the brachialis at the elbow. The biceps and brachialis function in the cocking phase to accomplish elbow flexion and also during follow through to decelerate the forearm. The triceps propel the forearm forward during acceleration and into follow-through (see Table 3.2).

Table 3.2

Muscles used in phases of throwing.

Cocking
Deltoid
Supraspinatus
Infraspinatus

Acceleration
Subscapularis
Pectoralis major
Latissimus dorsi
Teres major

Follow-through
Latissimus dorsi
Supraspinatus
Infraspinatus
Teres minor

4

Examination of the shoulder: how, when, where

The diagnosis and treatment of shoulder complaints begins with the history of injury. One must ask how, when, and where the injury occurred. The examiner should be fully cognizant of what the patient is stating and, therefore, should never interrupt.

Once the patient has presented his or her symptoms, specific leading questions should be asked regarding the patient's movements a few days to a week prior to the onset of pain or causes of pain aggravation or quiescence. This stage is necessary since what a patient may regard as normal activity in fact is often the inciting cause of the shoulder complaint.

The character of pain must be detailed since it is important to ascertain whether the pain is of acute onset or is progressive and chronic. Factors to determine include whether the pain occurred with an acute injury or from repetitive overuse; is the pain sharp, dull, constant, or intermittent in nature; is the pain present during the day, night, or at all times; is the pain in one spot or does it radiate or occur with certain arm motions. The medical history and review of systems must be included since shoulder pain can be secondary to other causes such as problems related to malignancy of the prostate, pelvic organs, breast (in females), kidney, and lungs. Diseases of the chest such as pneumonia, pulmonary embolism, and pleuritis can be inciting causes of referred shoulder pain. Diaphragmatic irritation from diseases of the abdominal cavity must be investigated.

Physical examination

In order to examine a patient properly, the chest and shoulder girdles must be exposed. Men must strip to the waist and women should have a gown that is open in the back in order to expose the upper body.

Inspection

Examination should be carried out in order to find evidence of atrophy, scars from previous surgery, and/or masses. The range and synchrony of motion should be noted and recorded as recommended by the American Academy of Orthopaedic Surgeons (1962) (*Figures 4.1–4.6*). The use of a goniometer is recommended for consistency in measurement of

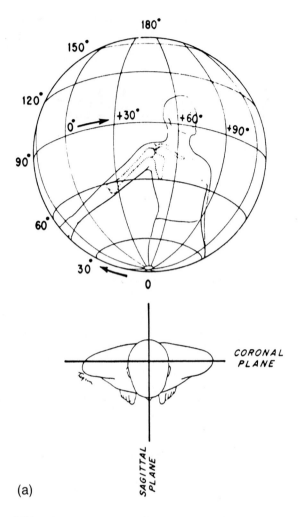

(a)

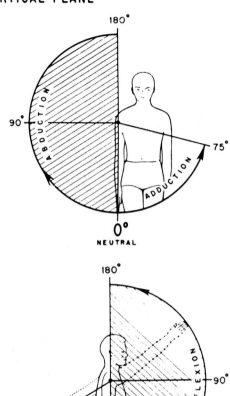

VERTICAL PLANE

HORIZONTAL PLANE

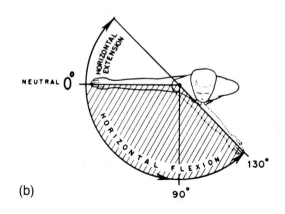

(b)

Figure 4.1

Methods of identification of planes of shoulder motion, according to the American Academy of Orthopaedic Surgeons (1962). (a) Global shoulder motion. (b) Vertical and horizontal motion. (c) Positions of elevation of the arm: A, neutral abduction; B, abduction in 45° of horizontal flexion; C, forward flexion; D, adduction in 135° of horizontal flexion; E, neutral adduction; F, backward extension; G, abduction in 45° of horizontal extension. (d) Inward (internal) and outward (external) rotation. (e) Motions of the cervical spine. (f) Motions of the shoulder girdle. (g) True glenohumeral motion and combined scapulothoracic motion. (Courtesy of Rowe 1988, pp. 58–60).

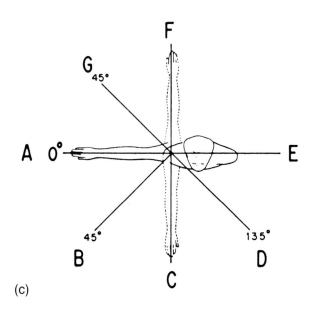

(c)

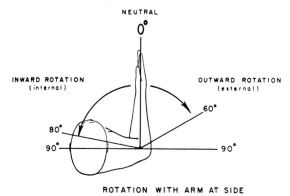

NEUTRAL
0°

INWARD ROTATION
(internal)

OUTWARD ROTATION
(external)
60°

80°
90°   90°

ROTATION WITH ARM AT SIDE

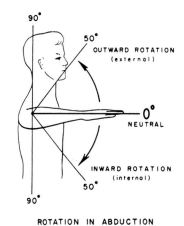

90°

50°
OUTWARD ROTATION
(external)

0°
NEUTRAL

INWARD ROTATION
(internal)
50°

90°

ROTATION IN ABDUCTION

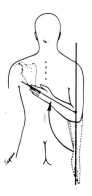

(d)   INTERNAL ROTATION
POSTERIORLY

Figure 4.1 (cont'd)

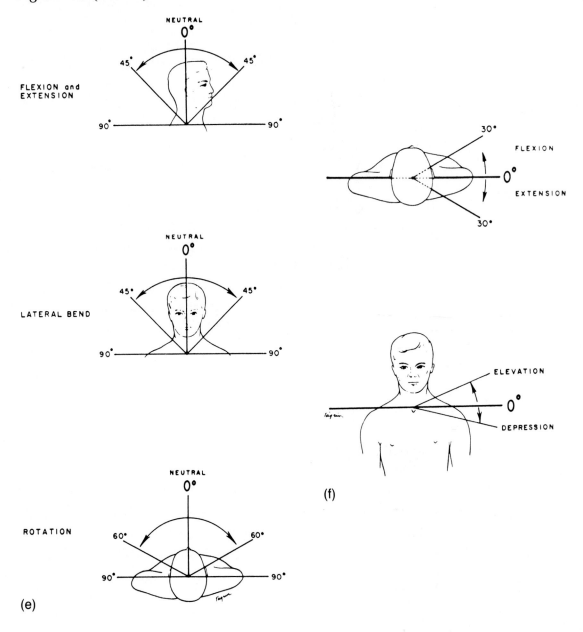

(e)

(f)

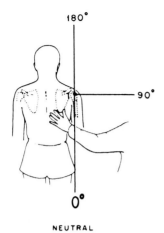

NEUTRAL

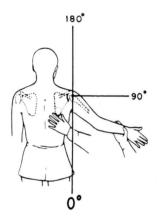

RANGE OF TRUE
GLENOHUMERAL MOTION

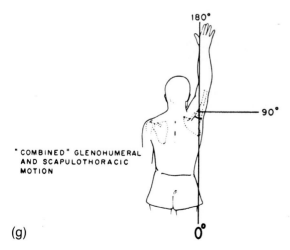

"COMBINED" GLENOHUMERAL
AND SCAPULOTHORACIC
MOTION

(g)

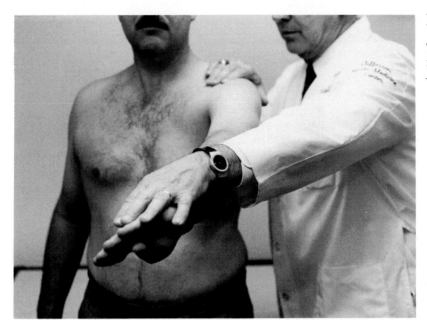

Figure 4.2

Testing strength in forward
motion.

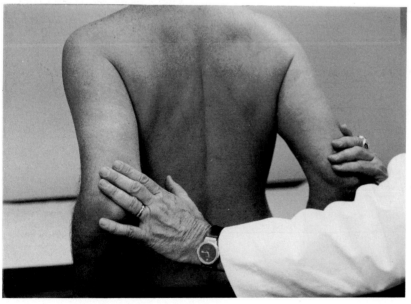

Figure 4.3

Testing bilateral backward
extension strength.

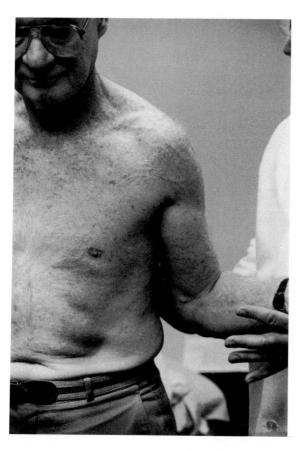

Figure 4.4

Testing external rotation strength.

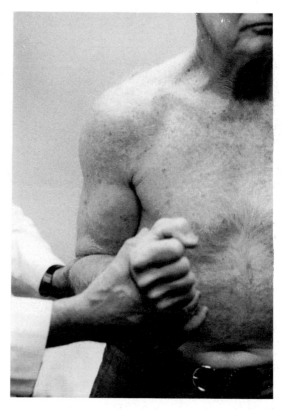

Figure 4.5

Testing internal rotation strength.

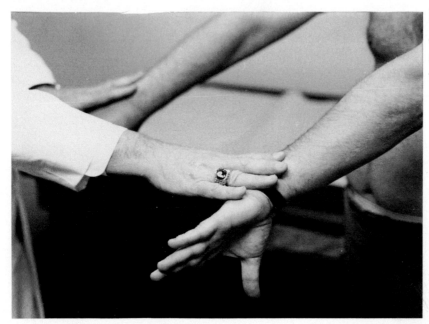

Figure 4.6

Testing bilateral
supraspinatus strength.

---

motions about the shoulder joint. The unaffected extremity must be evaluated and its motions recorded prior to examining and recording the affected extremity. One should look for a sulcus sign or step-off deformity indicating significant atrophy of the deltoid, inferior subluxation, dislocation, or multidirectional laxity.

Palpation

Palpation is an important part of the examination in order to detect evidence of decrease in bulk of the musculature and/or any specific areas of tenderness. The supraspinatus and infraspinatus fossa, the brachial plexus, the sternoclavicular and acromioclavicular joints, and surrounding musculature must all be palpated. The spinous process palpation of T2 through T10 is recommended and must be

part of the overall examination. The detection of areas of hypoesthesia, anesthesia, or hyperesthesia is important and must be noted.

Strength testing

Manual muscle testing is a necessary and important part of the complete examination of the upper extremity since it demonstrates which muscle groups are weak.

Muscle strength is rated from 0 to 5 with 0 being paralysis and 5 being normal or excellent. Rating 1 is a trace of function, and 2 is poor muscle function, while 3 is fair, and 4 is good. The musculature usually tested about the shoulder includes the three portions of the deltoid, the supraspinatus, infraspinatus, biceps, brachialis, triceps, trapezius, rhomboid, serratus anterior, and subscapularis.

5
Investigative techniques

Radiography

While there is no consensus on what constitutes an adequate radiographic examination of
the shoulder it would seem that in addition to
internal (*Figures 5.1, 5.2*) and external (*Figures 5.3, 5.4*) rotation views in the anteroposterior (AP) plane, it would be preferable to
rotate the patient into a 40° posterior oblique
view in order to have a true tangential view
(*Figures 5.5, 5.6*) of the glenohumeral joint.
The axillary view, originally described by
Lawrence (1918), offers the greatest amount of

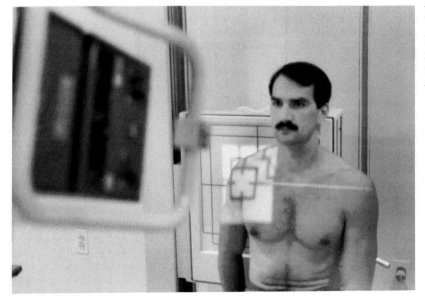

Figure 5.1

Positioning for internal
rotation view during
radiographic examination.

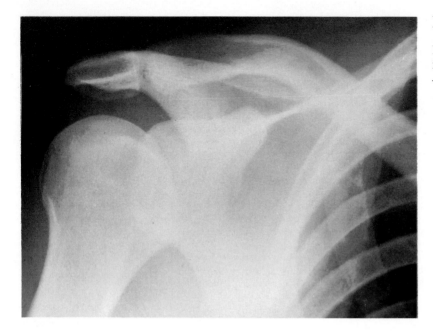

Figure 5.2

Radiographic view of
internal rotation.

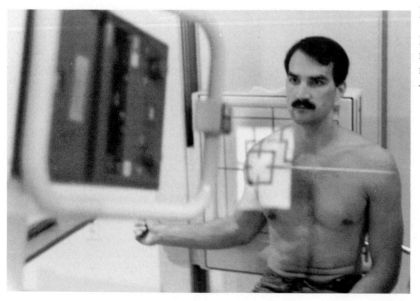

Figure 5.3

Positioning for external
rotation view during
radiographic examination.

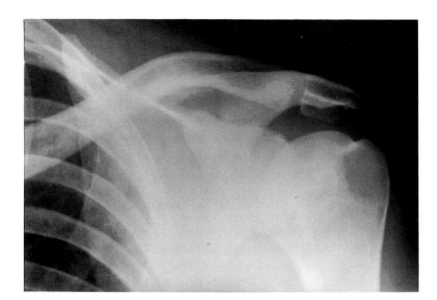

Figure 5.4

Radiographic view of external rotation.

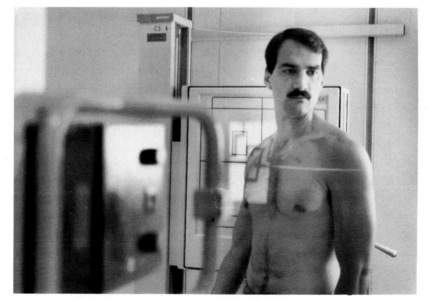

Figure 5.5

Positioning for tangential view with patient rotated into a 40° posterior oblique mode during radiographic examination.

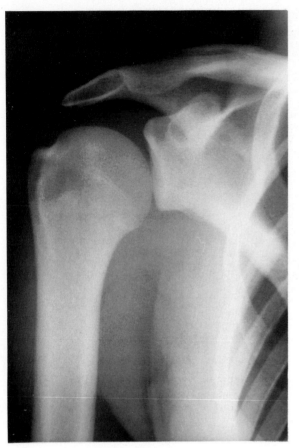

Figure 5.6

Radiographic tangential view demonstrating
glenohumeral joint with patient rotated posterior
obliquely 40°.

additional anatomic information and is preferred whenever it can be obtained (*Figures
5.7, 5.8*. It should be noted that positioning for
the axillary view may be difficult and painful,
particularly in patients who have sustained
acute shoulder injuries. In such patients, a Y
view (see below) a suitable alternative.

Views for special purposes

In an effort to evaluate shoulder instability,
subluxation, and dislocation, it is necessary to
test the degree of anterior or posterior
displacement of the humerus with respect to
the glenoid. This can be achieved most
directly using lateral or axial views, but it also
can be performed using AP or posteroanterior
(PA) images with cranial and caudal angulation.

Axillary projection

The axillary projection offers increased definition of the anatomy, but it may be difficult to
position the acutely injured patient for such
a view. For this reason, several modifications
of the axillary view have been devised.
The lateral recumbent axillary view requires
the patient to lie on the unaffected side and
requires less abduction of the arm than does
the conventional axillary view.

Anterior oblique views

The scapular Y view (*Figures 5.9, 5.10*) is an
effective method of diagnosing dislocation.
Correctly performed, the humeral head pro-
jects over the crotch of the 'Y' formed by the

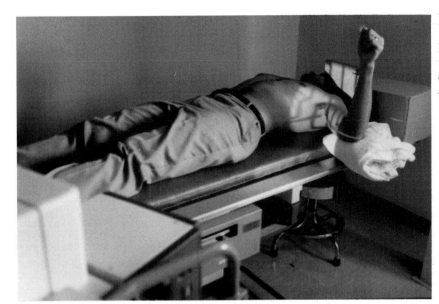

Figure 5.7

Positioning for axillary view during radiographic examination.

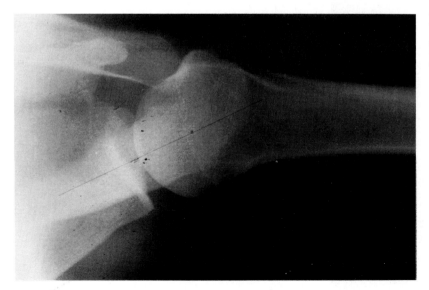

Figure 5.8

Radiographic axillary view.

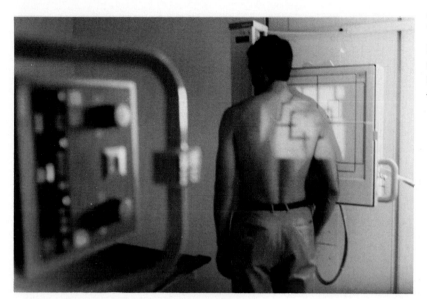

Figure 5.9

Positioning for Y view of
shoulder during
radiographic examination.

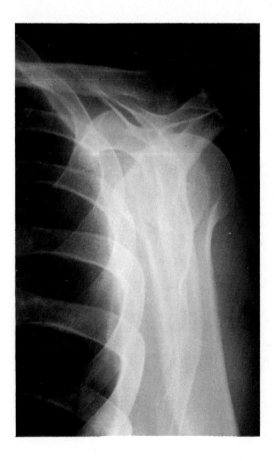

Figure 5.10

Radiographic result of Y view.

body of the scapula, the coracoid process, and the scapular spine. Anterior and posterior displacement are readily recognized.

At times, it is important to demonstrate by plain film a Hill–Sachs lesion, the coracoid process, and the acromioclavicular and sternoclavicular joints. Excellent results have been obtained with a 60° internal rotation view or a modified West Point axillary view.

A fracture of the anterior glenoid, which may accompany a Bankart lesion, is most consistently observed on the modified West Point axillary views. The conventional axillary view and the AP view in external rotation are also useful for this lesion.

The acromioclavicular joint is best evaluated using AP views obtained with cephalad beam angulation. These views should be angled 12–15° or 30–35° towards the head (*Figures 5.11, 5.12*).

The coracoid process can be difficult to see on the AP view, therefore most authors recommend the use of axillary projections for demonstration of coracoid fractures. Views with 30–35° of cephalad angulation have been shown to be effective in the diagnosis of fractures of the base of the coracoid (*Figures 5.13, 5.14*).

The sternoclavicular joints are extremely difficult to demonstrate. A 50° oblique view and lateral views may be helpful, but additional studies will be necessary.

Plain X-rays are virtually inadequate for injuries other than for acute dislocations and/or fractures that are quite evident. Other imaging techniques such as computed tomography (CT) (*Figure 5.15*), plain or CT arthrography (*Figure 5.16*), ultrasonography (*Figure 5.17*), and most recently MRI (*Figure 5.18*) techniques are therefore relied upon.

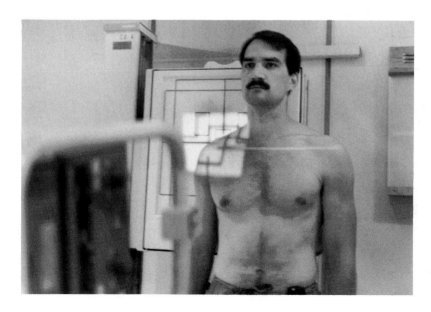

Figure 5.11

Positioning utilizing 15° cephalad beam angulation for radiographic evaluation of acromioclavicular joint.

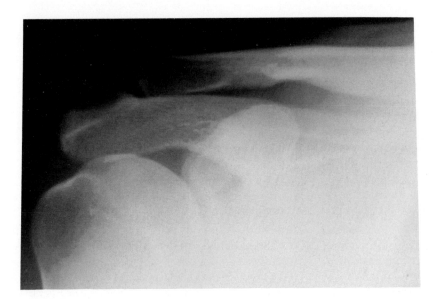

Figure 5.12

Radiographic view of normal acromioclavicular view.

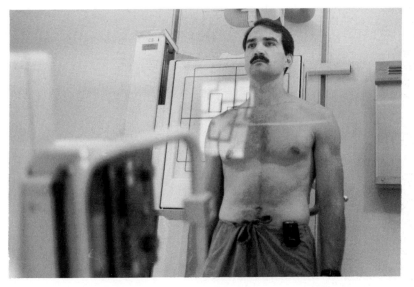

Figure 5.13

Positioning to demonstrate fracture at base of coracoid of shoulder utilizing 30° cephalad beam angulation.

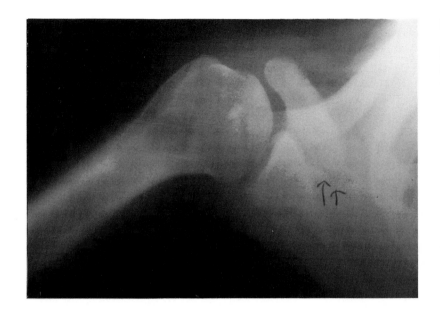

Figure 5.14

Fracture at base of coracoid process.

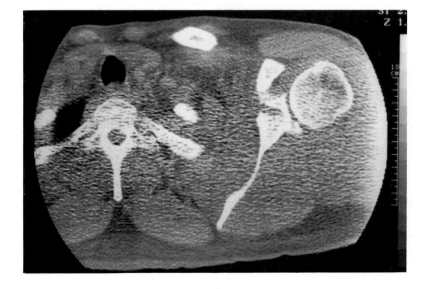

Figure 5.15

Normal CT scan of the shoulder.

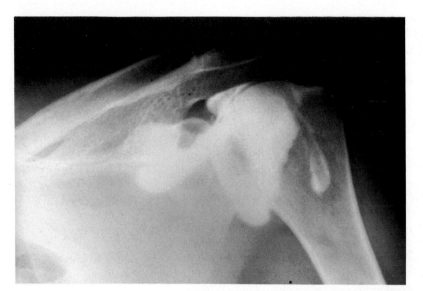

Figure 5.16

Normal arthrogram of the
shoulder, demonstrating
absence of a rotator cuff
tear.

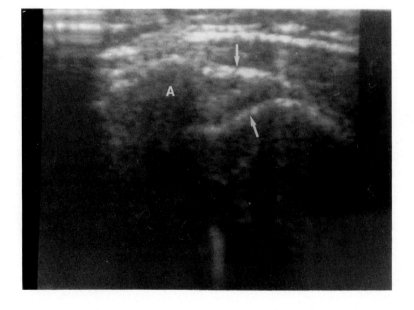

Figure 5.17

Longitudinal ultrasonogram
of a well-defined
supraspinatus tendon
(arrows), lateral to the
acromium shadow (A).

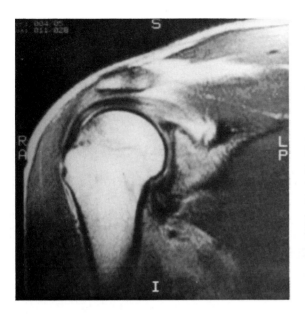

Figure 5.18

Normal MRI scan.

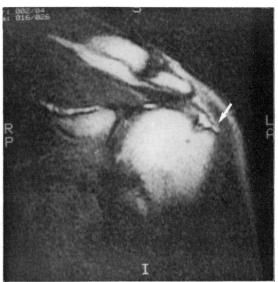

Figure 5.19

MRI scan demonstrating cystic changes (arrow) at greater tuberosity with rotator cuff tear.

Magnetic resonance imaging

The modality of MRI is especially promising in that it reveals more than previously has been observed with other imaging techniques. Articular cartilage lesions, loose bodies, rotator cuff tears, strains of other tendons such as the teres major and latissimus dorsi, soft-tissue tumors, impingement syndromes, and fluid in and about the shoulder joint, are all detected with MRI.

In a recently published article by Burk et al (1991), MRI was utilized to evaluate shoulders of 10 symptomatic professional baseball players and one asymptomatic player. There was surgical correlation in six cases, with arthrographic correlation in two cases. Seven small rotator cuff tears measuring 0.5–1 cm were identified on MRI images, with arthrographic and surgical confirmation of these findings in two patients and surgical confirmation in three. Cortical irregularity and/or subchondral cyst formation (*Figure 5.19*) at the posterior aspect of the greater tuberosity near the insertion site of the infraspinatus tendon were found in five of the seven players with rotator cuff tears (*Figure 5.21*). Similar findings were noted in an asymptomatic volunteer and in one of the three players without a cuff tear.

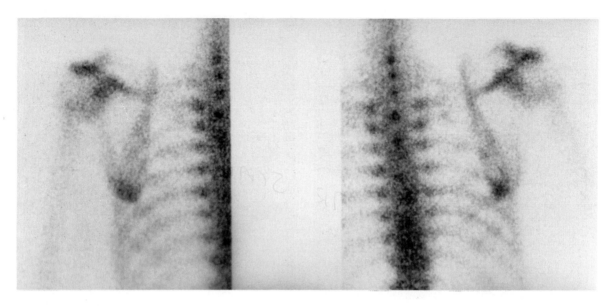

Figure 5.20

Bone scan, demonstrating slight increased uptake
in left glenohumeral joint, consistent with
synovitis.

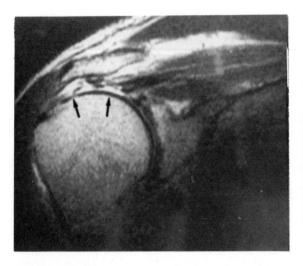

Figure 5.21

MRI scan, demonstrating complete or high-grade
partial tear (arrows) of left supraspinatus tendon
proximal to its insertion on the greater tuberosity.

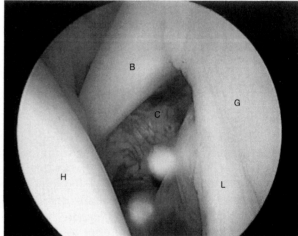

Figure 5.22

Arthroscopic view revealing normal glenohumeral
joint, depicting humerus (H), glenoid (G), biceps
tendon (B), labrum (L) and capsule (C).

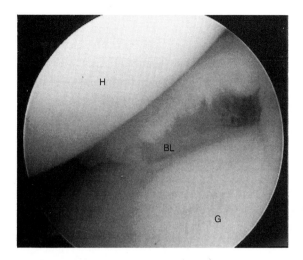

Figure 5.23

Arthroscopic view revealing humeral head (H), glenoid (G) and a Bankart lesion (BL).

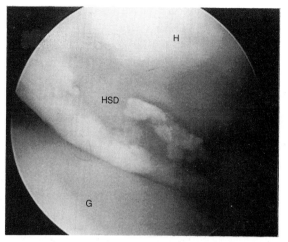

Figure 5.24

Arthroscopic view depicting glenoid (G) and humeral head (H), revealing a Hill–Sachs deformity (HSD).

Bone scans

A bone scan of the shoulder girdle (*Figure 5.20*) is an important investigative technique, and is particularly so when looking for the following:

- tumors about the shoulder girdle

- acromioclavicular arthritis

- osteolysis of the clavicle

- stress fractures of the proximal humerus, and/or coracoid process

- synovitis of the glenohumeral joint

Arthroscopy

Examination of the glenohumeral joint, the subacromial space, and the acromioclavicular area is easily demonstrated via the arthroscopic route (*Figures 5.22–5.24*). At present, diagnostic shoulder arthroscopy is well established and has a definite place in the diagnosis of shoulder conditions. Arthroscopy should be utilized in the following conditions:

- if a thorough, complete history and physical examination, coupled with the evaluative techniques as described previously, do not indicate why there is pain or abnormal motion in the shoulder

- to inspect the rotator cuff from above and below in patients who have painful subacromial impingement

- to confirm or rule out the glenohumeral joint as the site of pathology in patients who have atypical shoulder pain

- to obtain tissue or fluid under direct visualization, or to remove loose bodies

The technique of arthroscopy has been previously described thoroughly in the literature and therefore is not detailed in this book; however, it should be noted that there are two basic arthroscopic positions utilized: the lateral decubitus position and the barber-chair position. There are certain advantages of the barber chair over the lateral decubitus position; however, the surgeon must be comfortable in whichever position is utilized. The advantages of the barber-chair position are as follows:

- it enables the patient's arm to hang down freely, and gravity provides enough force to open up the shoulder joint

- the surgeon can manipulate the shoulder when desired

- it requires less time to position patients

- arthroscopic acromioplasty is more easily accomplished, since the arm is in a neutral position maximizing the subacromial space

- if an open procedure is necessary following arthroscopy, the barber-chair position allows the surgeon to proceed directly to the surgery without breaking sterility

- there is no need for an assistant

- triangulation is easier to perform

A number of complications of shoulder arthroscopy have been reported and are summarized herein. The rate of complications associated with shoulder arthroscopy is relatively low; however, when a complication occurs it can be devastating. Many complications may go either undetected or underreported and therefore the true complication rate is most likely to be higher than stated.

The pitfalls in shoulder arthroscopy are as follows:

- proper entry into the shoulder joint is the most difficult aspect of the procedure. A thorough knowledge of the surface landmarks of the shoulder is essential in performing the operation safely

- irrigation fluid extravasates easily from the joint, thus limiting the usefulness of positive-pressure pumps

- intraoperative bleeding cannot be controlled by a tourniquet. Anterior portals, when required, should avoid placement too far medially or inferiorly. The intra-articular triangle, bordered by the glenoid fossa, the humeral head, and the biceps tendon, is used as a guide to transilluminate the anterior soft tissues and the anterior portal

- neurologic complications occur when either the brachial plexus anteriorly or the axillary nerve posteriorly, is speared

- improper localization can cause defects in the humeral head and/or glenoid cavity

- there is breakage of material such as staples when used in stapling procedures about the shoulder for recurrent subluxation or dislocation

- infection rates are low, ranging from 0.4 to 3.4 percent

Electrodiagnostic studies

Electrodiagnostic studies are objective and therefore not under the control of patients with regard to the outcome. The studies should be performed by an individual who is adept in reproduction of results and has the ability to eliminate technical errors and misinterpretations. When ordering electro-diagnostic studies, the physician must communicate with the electromyographer. This is necessary so that he or she understands what is being investigated.

The studies indicate whether a muscle is normal or affected by neurogenic or myopathic processes. Electrodiagnostic studies have the ability to state whether the problem is acute or chronic in onset and can localize the area of involvement from the spinal column to the distal end of the peripheral nerve. The types of electrodiagnostic studies commonly used are electromyography, nerve-conduction velocity determination, and F responses. While it is not the purpose of this book to discuss the details of the techniques of electromyography, it is necessary to describe what can be determined by the various studies.

Electromyography

Electromyography determines whether a muscle is partially or completely denervated. Partial denervation has the appearance of low-voltage potential, with larger units causing sharp positive waves, not all of which are under the patient's voluntary control. If a muscle is totally denervated, there are no voluntary potentials seen on attempted contraction. Muscle that is atrophied due to disuse will not demonstrate fibrillation potentials and sharp positive waves at rest. Likewise, there will not be a high percentage of polyphasic units, as is observed in a muscle that is partially denervated (*Figure 5.25*).

Nerve-conduction velocity determination

Localization of a nerve lesion along the course of a limb can be determined by measurement of the velocity of conduction of the peripheral nerve (*Figure 5.26*). Nerve-conduction velocity determination requires percutaneous stimulation of a nerve at least at two points along its course. Therefore, it is far more suited for use below the axilla than about the shoulder. The determination of latency — that is, the interval between the stimulus of a nerve and the response from the muscle — may be of value if the contralateral side is normal.

The F response

Since conventional nerve-conduction studies have limited application to proximal nerve lesions, motor conduction along the proximal segment can be measured by the use of the F wave. This is a late muscle potential that is elicited from antidromically activated anterior horn cells. A stimulus is applied trans-cutaneously to the motor nerve in the hand, which travels centrally to the level of the anterior horn cell. An impulse is then transmitted antidromically down the motor nerve to the muscle. It is a late potential, the latency of which depends on the length of the nerve between the point of stimulation and the spinal cord. In combination with conventional nerve-conduction velocity determinations, it may be used to define more proximal and largely inaccessible areas of the neuraxis, such as the brachial plexus and the region of the spinal nerve roots. Brachial plexus injuries, whether they be complete or incomplete, a brachial plexus neuritis, the thoracic outlet syndrome, cervical radiculopathy, supra-scapular nerve involvement, the long thoracic nerve involvement, axillary nerve involvement, and spinal accessory nerve problems can be determined with EMG (*Figure 5.27*).

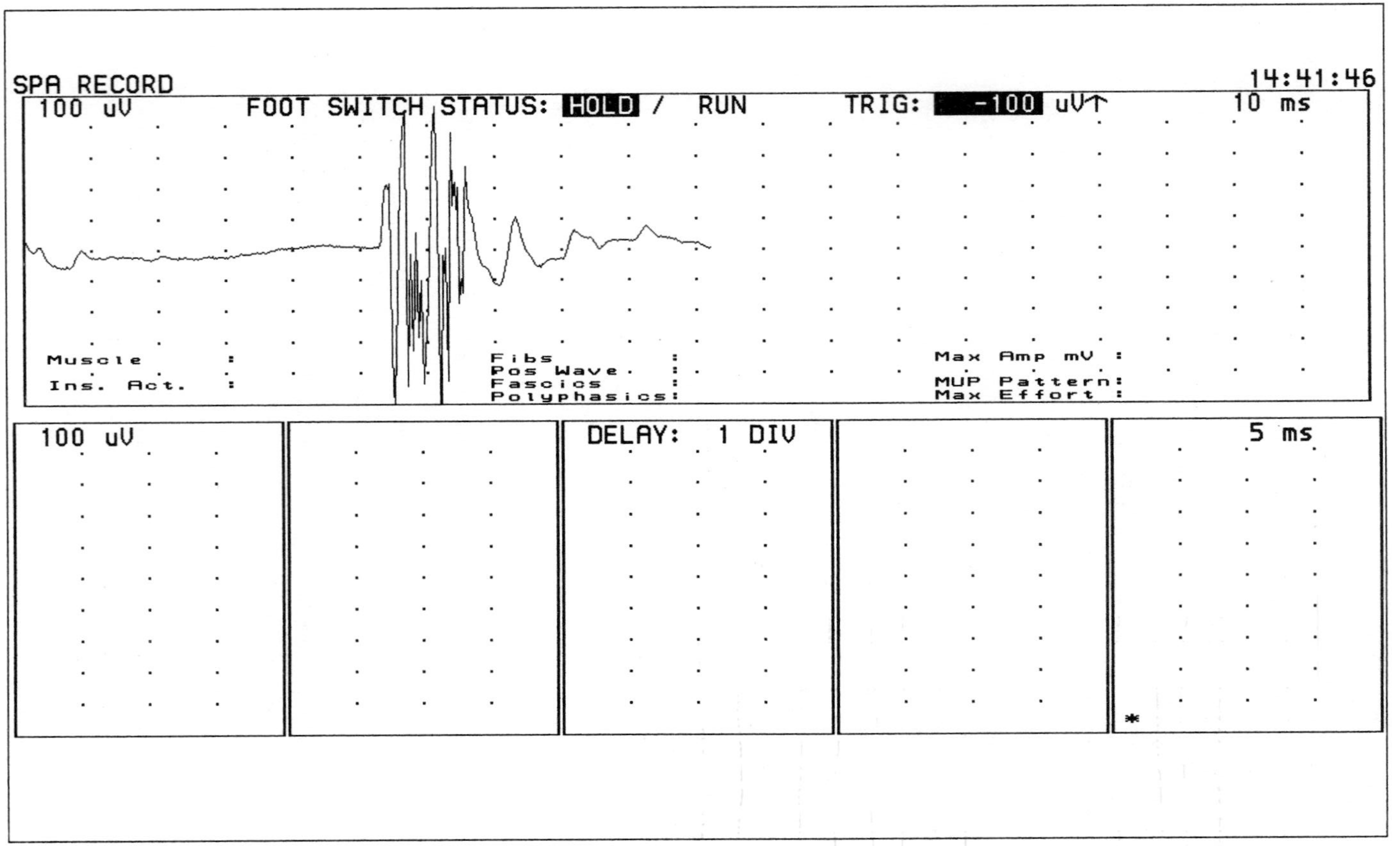

Figure 5.25

Electromyograph: polyphasic motor unit (courtesy of Richard L. Read, PT, ECS, Hand Rehabilitation Center Ltd, Philadelphia, Pennsylvania).

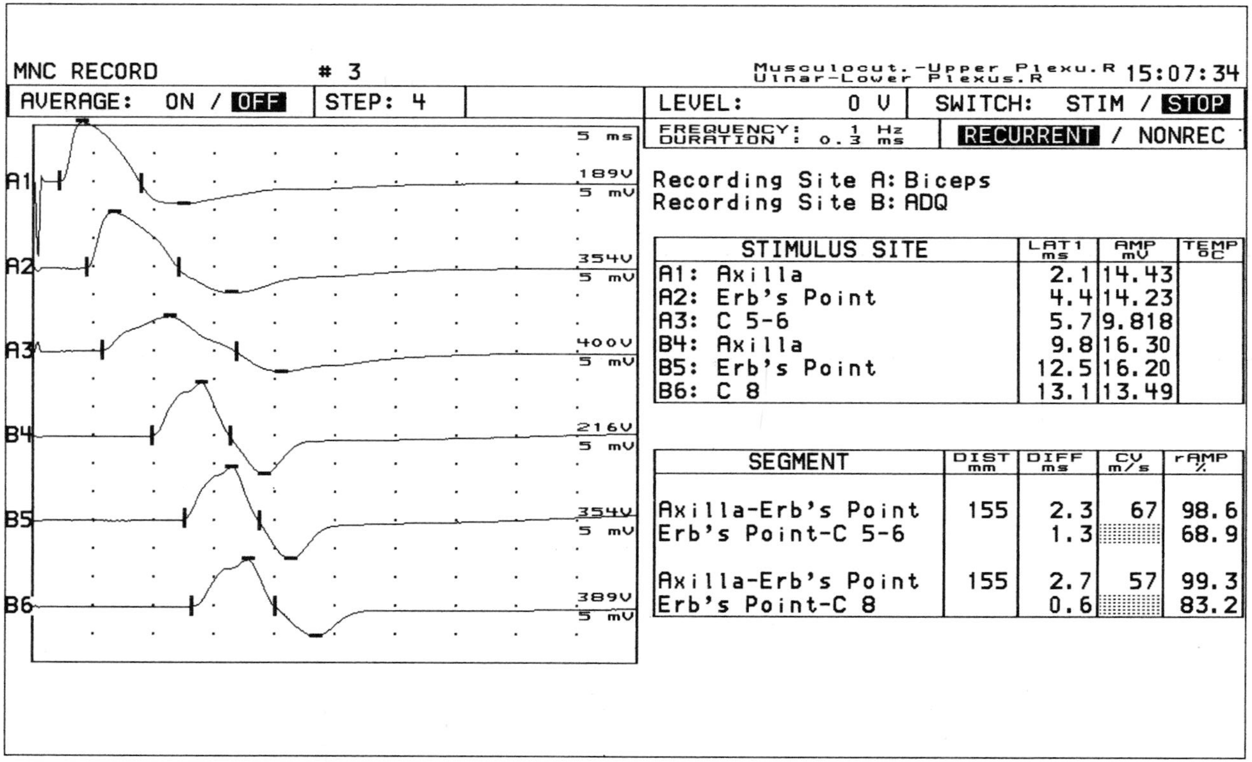

MNC RECORD   # 3   STEP: 4

Musolocut.-Upper Plexu.R 15:07:34
Ulnar-Lower Plexus.R

AVERAGE: ON / **OFF**

LEVEL: 0 V   SWITCH: STIM / **STOP**

FREQUENCY: 0.1 Hz
DURATION: 0.3 ms   **RECURRENT** / NONREC

Recording Site A: Biceps
Recording Site B: ADQ

STIMULUS SITE	LAT¹ ms	AMP mU	TEMP °C
A1: Axilla	2.1	14.43	
A2: Erb's Point	4.4	14.23	
A3: C 5-6	5.7	9.818	
B4: Axilla	9.8	16.30	
B5: Erb's Point	12.5	16.20	
B6: C 8	13.1	13.49	

SEGMENT	DIST mm	DIFF ms	CV m/s	rAMP %
Axilla-Erb's Point	155	2.3	67	98.6
Erb's Point-C 5-6		1.3		68.9
Axilla-Erb's Point	155	2.7	57	99.3
Erb's Point-C 8		0.6		83.2

A1 189V / 5 mV   5 ms
A2 354V / 5 mV
A3 400V / 5 mV
B4 216V / 5 mV
B5 354V / 5 mV
B6 389V / 5 mV

Figure 5.26

Nerve-conduction velocity: the scan shows
conduction across the upper lung (C5–6 to
triceps) and the lower plexus medial cord (axilla
to Erb's point) (courtesy of Richard L. Read, PT,
ECS, Hand Rehabilitation Center Ltd,
Philadelphia, Pennsylvania).

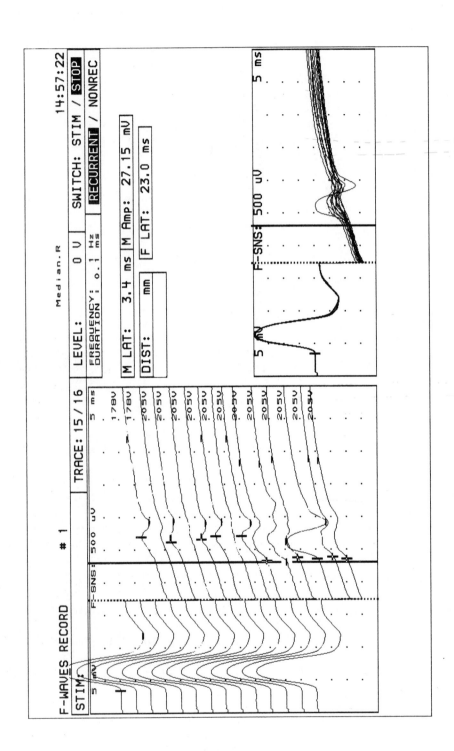

Figure 5.27

The F response (courtesy of Richard L. Read, PT, ECS, Hand Rehabilitation Center Ltd, Philadelphia, Pennsylvania).

6

An overview of injuries affecting the shoulder girdle

Acute traumatic injuries

Fractures

Fractures of the shoulder girdle account for approximately 45 percent of all fractures of the body, being very common in adults and less common in children. Fortunately, 80 percent of proximal humeral fractures are minimally displaced, and satisfactory results can be obtained with nonoperative treatment.

Fractures of the clavicle are the most common fractures of the shoulder girdle; those of the glenoid rim, the tuberosity of the humerus, and the body of the scapula are less common.

Proximal humeral physeal separation occurs in skeletally immature baseball players, particularly so in males between the age of 11 and 15 years, who have been pitching extensively. Symptoms include shoulder pain, with the inability to throw with velocity. Radiographs typically demonstrate physeal widening but can also show minimal displacement (*Figure 6.1*). Treatment includes temporary cessation of pitching. The outcome is uniformly satisfactory.

Football injuries commonly occur about the shoulder girdle and are usually due to falls.

The frequency of shoulder injury is probably secondary only to the knee in professional football players. In studies of injuries in high-school and college football, the incidence of shoulder injuries was found to be high, with only the knee and ankle joint more frequently involved. The clavicle is the most commonly fractured bone in football injuries.

Direct trauma to the shoulder is the most usual cause of fractures in ice-hockey players. Norfray et al (1977) demonstrated that 46 per cent of professional hockey players had radiologic abnormalities of the clavicle. Acute clavicular fractures were the most common problem in amateur players. Post-traumatic changes of the distal end of the clavicle were seen in professional hockey players; the radiologic abnormalities included widening of the acromioclavicular joint, ununited fracture fragments, and exuberant callus.

Stress fractures of the coracoid process have been referred to as 'trapshooter's shoulder'; however, this injury occurred in a professional baseball pitcher who initially complained of discomfort in and about the shoulder girdle. On one occasion, while throwing a pitch, he experienced acute disabling pain. The radiographic examination, with a 30° cephalad view, revealed a fracture of the base of

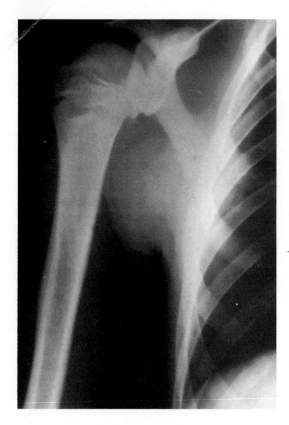

Figure 6.1

Radiographic view demonstrating physeal widening or 'little league shoulder'.

the coracoid process (*Figure 6.2*). Acute coracoid fracture occurs usually in individuals who sustain significant trauma and includes fractures of the distal clavicle and/or severe chest trauma, constituting a surgical emergency for the nonclavicular trauma.

Stress fractures of the proximal humerus are commonly seen in baseball players who, during the throwing motion, will complain of a dull ache in the arm as a prodrome. Acute excruciating pain occurs followed by the inability to function secondary to a spiral fracture of the proximal shaft of the humerus (*Figure 6.3*).

While most fractures about the shoulder heal with time and avoidance of active participation in sports, some necessitate operative intervention, particularly those at the distal end of the clavicle or those with large fragments from the glenoid rim of the scapula (*Figure 6.4*).

The treatment of clavicular fractures varies from the use of a sling alone or combined with a figure-of-eight cloth dressing, to plaster immobilization. It is the author's preference that reduction followed by plaster immobilization is the method of treatment since this technique interferes less with the axillary area, thus avoiding swelling, cyanosis, and tingling of the upper extremity, while maintaining the reduction and sufficient length of the clavicle. These latter considerations are particularly important in individuals, such as baseball pitchers, involved in throwing sports, since any posthealing problem such as excessive callus or shortening of the clavicle must be precluded. If healing occurs with shortening or excessive callus, it could cause brachial plexus irritation, interference with vascular supply, possible effort thrombosis, and asynchronous motion of the shoulder girdle.

Dislocations

Dislocations of the shoulder joint are common in sport injuries, particularly so with contact

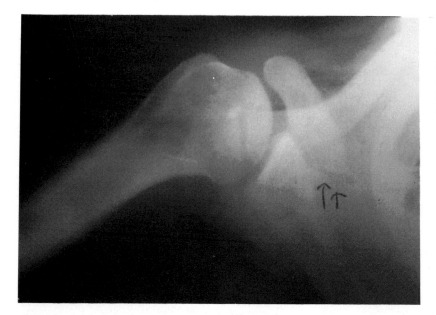

Figu 50

Radio
demo
corac
shoul___ (_____).

sports. While anterior dislocation is the most common shoulder dislocation, posterior dislocation, while not common, is frequently misdiagnosed. Shoulder dislocations in baseball players are rather uncommon; however, a significant number occur in basketball players. Anterior shoulder dislocation is not so unusual in competitive high divers since it occurs at water entry as the result of divers not clasping their hands prior to entry, therefore forcibly hyperextending and externally rotating the shoulder. A significant number of shoulder injuries occur in football and ice hockey, and dislocation of the shoulder also occurs with a reasonably high frequency. In a study of elite ice-hockey players in Sweden, Hovelius (1978) found that the incidence of primary glenohumeral dislocation was 8 per-

cent. More than 90 percent of players over 20 years old had recurrence of dislocation.

Treatment of anterior shoulder dislocation is reduction of the dislocation, followed by immobilization until pain disappears; however, isometric exercises are begun immediately. Once the pain is relieved motion below the horizontal commences. At approximately four weeks, motion above the horizontal can be instituted without fear of increasing the incidence of redislocation since recurrent dislocation is not dependent upon the total length of immobilization following the initial dislocation. Some physicians have reported the recurrent dislocation rate to be as high as 90 percent in the young active athlete; they advocate the use of immediate acute repair of the initial dislocation,

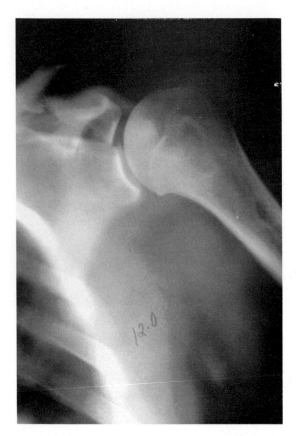

Figure 6.4

Radiographic view demonstrating large fracture
fragment of glenoid rim of scapula.

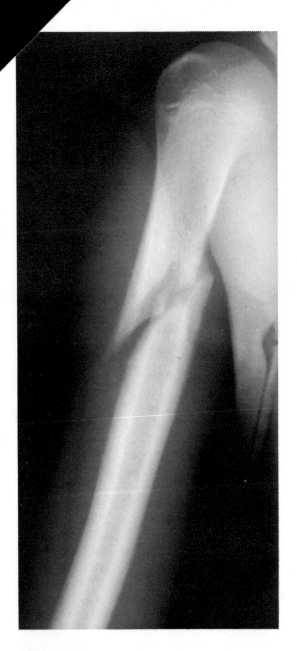

Figure 6.3

Radiographic view demonstrating spiral fracture
of humerus incurred during act of throwing.

particularly if a Bankart lesion exists. The author does not subscribe to this plan of treatment and will not do so until further evidence has demonstrated a significant statistical reduction in the recurrence rate with surgery. It will be noted in Chapter 10 that Dr Craig Morgan of Wilmington, Delaware, has experience with immediate repair of acute dislocations, utilizing an arthroscopic technique. He is currently involved in a prospective study of acute repair; however, the results are not known at present.

Subluxations

Subluxation of the shoulder, usually anterior, may occur on an acute traumatic basis. As in acute dislocations, it may go on to cause functional disability because of pain and altered mechanics, particularly in those involved in throwing sports. A rehabilitative exercise program as outlined in Chapter 14 is suggested and should be followed after the initial and possibly second and third episodes. If this fails, anterior capsular repair should be performed. The author's preferred type of repair is a capsular repair.

Posterior subluxation of the shoulder, while not as common as anterior subluxation, is actually more prevalent than previously reported. It is of grave concern in the throwing athlete. A conservative exercise program is the preferred treatment for this problem. Special emphasis is placed upon the external rotators so that they can be selectively strengthened in conjunction with a program for strengthening the shoulder girdle musculature. If this program fails, surgery is indicated for the elite athlete wherein a posterior capsular shift is the method of choice. The author cautions the reader that this procedure is not to be taken lightly and should only be per-

formed in athletes who a active, whose goal is profe rationale for this statemen ficial results of an operativ compare with those for an

Acute brachial plexus stretch injuries

An acute brachial plexus stretch injury is an acute injury to the plexus that causes sharp burning pain radiating from the shoulder to the arm and hand. It is caused by a blow that tilts the head and neck away from the side of injury, accompanied with depression of the shoulder (*Figure 6.5*). A burning paresthesia, usually lasting several seconds, is followed by arm and hand weakness that can last 1–2 minutes. The etiology of this injury is an excessive stretching of the brachial plexus and should be distinguished from injury to the cervical spine nerve roots and an acute shoulder impingement injury. If the brachial plexus has been stretched, the nerves innervating the biceps, deltoid, supraspinatus or infraspinatus are usually involved. In cervical spine nerve root injuries, C5 is commonly involved. If the pain lasts for more than a few seconds, and if the neck and upper extremity do not return to normal within one or two minutes, it should be assumed that the cervical spine and/or brachial plexus have been injured severely, until proven otherwise. It is imperative that radiographic examination of the cervical spine and shoulder girdle is provided as quickly as possible. Treatment is avoidance of the sport, use of a sling, and exercise. The prognosis is excellent, with a 90 percent recovery rate within 3–4 months if proper treatment guidelines are followed.

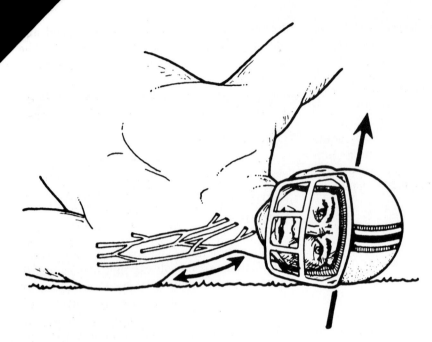

Figure 6.5

Action inducing brachial plexus stretch injury (courtesy of Rowe 1988, p. 419).

Strains

Acute strains occur about the shoulder as the result of overstretching mechanisms associated with a sudden rotational force. These are particularly painful and are accompanied with immediate loss of motion about the joint. Diagnostic studies do not reveal evidence of fracture or dislocation, and these strains are therefore treated with time, patience, rest, and administration of anti-inflammatory agents. Occasionally, the judicious use of steroids on a decreasing dose schedule over a six-day period is useful. A rehabilitation program prior to returning to active playing status is encouraged.

Sprains

A sprain is a tearing of the ligamentous fibers surrounding the shoulder joint. These are common in and about the acromioclavicular, sternoclavicular, and glenohumeral joints.

Sprains are classified as first-degree, second-degree, and third-degree, depending upon the amount of stretching of ligaments. First- or second-degree sprains of the acromioclavicular or sternoclavicular joint are treated without surgical intervention and the response is usually very gratifying since motion and strength return to normal. Third-degree sprains of the sternoclavicular joint, that is, a complete dislocation, are treated conservatively if they are of the anterior variety. They heal without significant decrease in strength and leave no functional disability.

A posterior sternoclavicular dislocation is a true medical emergency and must be reduced quickly. At times, a reduction can be effected with a closed technique; however, the surgeon should always be prepared to open, reduce, and fix the clavicle to the sternum surgically. If a pin is utilized, it should be of the threaded variety so that it does not advance. The third-degree acromioclavicular sprain, also known as a shoulder separation, can be treated nonoperatively with gratifying results. This is particularly true on the nondominant side. Some physicians feel that an acute repair of the dominant complete acromioclavicular dislocation is imperative; the author, however, does not agree with this. The overall results are encouraging and it has been demonstrated that if the acromioclavicular joint is not repaired, strength is not lost, and function is normal. **Third-degree acromioclavicular dislocations should be treated nonoperatively**.

Chronic overuse problems

The joints and articulations involved with shoulder motion are the sternoclavicular joint, the acromioclavicular joint, the glenohumeral joint, the scapulothoracic articulation, and the suprahumeral articulation of coracoacromial arch. These are subjected to a myriad of chronic repetitive injuries sometimes referred to as microtraumatic or overuse syndromes.

Stress fractures

Stress fractures are relatively common types of overuse syndromes in the shoulder area,

particularly in throwing sports. The most common types of stress fractures are those that occur in the immature individual, that is, the growing child. The little leaguers' shoulder or the 'physeal separation' is seen in active young pitchers (*Figure 6.6*). In adults, stress fractures occur and have been reported involving the coracoid process in tennis players and trapshooters, and unreported but personally treated by the author, in a professional baseball pitcher. These stress fractures heal without the need for surgery. Treatment is avoidance of activity, with motion commencing as the pain subsides. Isometric exercises in the acute phase are encouraged and are followed by graduated resistive exercises of the shoulder girdle when pain permits.

Stress fractures of the proximal humeral shaft are common in throwing sports, particularly in baseball pitchers. Minimal displacement is the rule and treatment is immobilization with an early rehabilitation program.

Rupture of the pectoralis major muscle

The pectoralis major muscle arises as a broad sheet in two divisions, each of which remains separate throughout its course. The upper half arises from the medial part of the clavicle and upper portion of the sternum, while the inferior portion arises from the distal end of the sternum and true ribs. The tendons twist on each other 90° at their insertion site on the humerus so that the sternal portion of the pectoralis inserts posterior to the clavicular portion. Due to this division, complete ruptures of the pectoralis major infrequently occur. Ruptures, complete or incomplete, of the pectoralis occur with direct trauma, the excessive stress and strain of weight training, or on occasions, when attempting to prevent a fall. The rupture occurs within the muscle belly, by avulsion of its tendinous insertion or by separation of its musculotendinous junc-

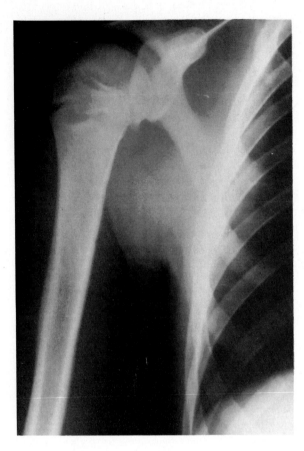

Figure 6.6

Radiographic view demonstrating physeal separation.

tion (*Figures 6.7, 6.8*). The results of the treatment depend on the portion of the muscle injury. Early surgical repair is recommended for the distal tendinous injuries while conservative therapy is advocated for disruptions of the muscle fibers. Rupture of the pectoralis major muscle probably occurs more frequently than reports indicate.

Sprains

The glenohumeral joint is involved more than any other area of the shoulder girdle in overuse problems. Although overuse sprains of the acromioclavicular joint and sternoclavicular joint may occur, these are uncommon. More commonly, these areas are involved with an inflammatory process such as osteolysis of the acromioclavicular joint or a thickening, swelling, and hyperemia of the surface area of the sternoclavicular joint. Treatment consists of time, anti-inflammatory agents, and a rehabilitative program. If the symptoms persist, a resection of the distal clavicle is the treatment of choice for acromioclavicular osteolysis (*Figure 6.9*).

The glenohumeral joint is the most common area involved with subluxation, with the most common subluxation being anterior. It should be noted there are a significant number of individuals involved in throwing sports with posterior subluxation. Multidirectional instability occurs with the added dimension of an inferior subluxation to anterior and posterior subluxation.

Anterior instability

Anterior instability is commonly seen in sporting activities such as throwing sports (especially baseball), swimming (particularly common in backstrokers), diving, football, ice hockey, weightlifting, and wrestling. Once the

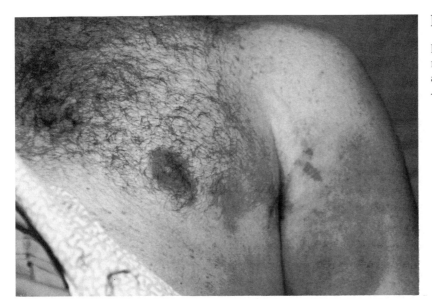

Figure 6.7

Rupture of pectoralis major muscle with ecchymosis in and about shoulder girdle.

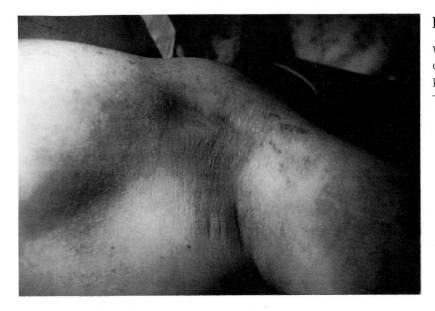

Figure 6.8

With arm adducted, a defect is seen in the pectoralis tendon.

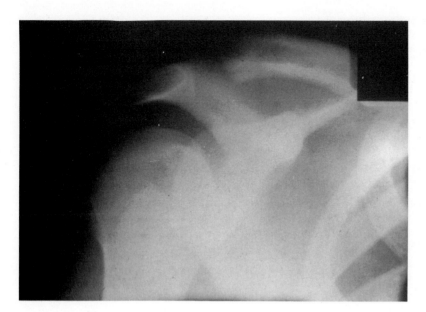

Figure 6.9

Radiographic view of
ressected distal clavicle for
acromioclavicular
osteolysis.

diagnosis is made, the treatment is directed towards decreasing the pain by stopping the activity which is causing it; the use of non-steroidal anti-inflammatory agents, heat and ice where indicated; and the commencement of a rehabilitative process as outlined in Chapter 14.

If the problem persists, a repair of the anterior part of the shoulder is indicated; however, it must be cautioned that those involved in throwing sports may never return to their previous level of activity.

Posterior instability

As discussed earlier, posterior subluxation of the shoulder is more prevalent than previously described. This is particularly so in throwing sports. The complaint is usually that of posterior shoulder pain; however, at times there may be anterior shoulder pain or pain in the posterior axillary fold (the area of the infraspinatus and teres minor musculature). Radiographically, evidence of hypertrophic bone formation in the posterior glenoid area, that is, Bennett's lesion, may be reserved (*Figure 6.10*). Magnetic resonance imaging reveals sclerosis and cyst formation in the area of the posterior facet of the greater tuberosity insertion of the infraspinatus tendon. Treatment is designed to include decrease of pain by cessation of the activity, the use of nonsteroidal anti-inflammatory agents and, occasionally, administration of steroids on a decreasing dose schedule over six days. This is supplemented with a rehabilitative program. The gradual resumption of the throwing act is as outlined in Chapter 14.

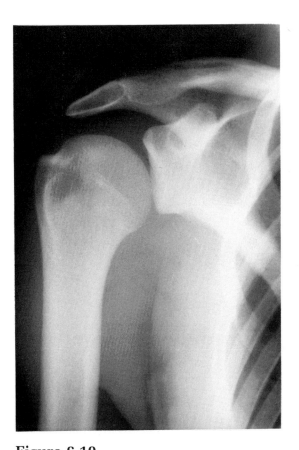

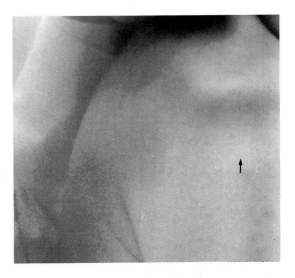

Figure 6.11

Sulcus sign indicating inferior shoulder subluxation (arrow).

Figure 6.10

Radiographic view of Bennett's lesion, demonstrated by hypertrophic bone formation in posterior glenoid area.

Multidirectional instability

Multidirectional instability is easy to diagnose, but difficult to treat. On examination, there is an inferior sulcus sign, as well as anterior or posterior laxity (*Figure 6.11*). Treatment of this condition is difficult and should be that of an intensive exercise program to regain muscle tone in and about the shoulder. In the author's experience, a return to a high level of throwing sports is suspect and probably will never occur for a sustained period of time. Surgery is not the treatment of choice of these individuals and, as far as the author is concerned, should never be performed unless recurrent dislocation occurs. The patient must be counseled as to the liabilities of this problem and also be made aware that surgery is rarely indicated.

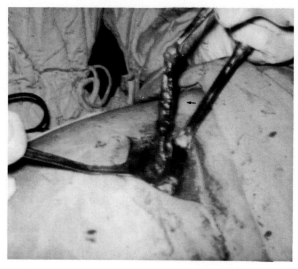

Figure 6.12

Adventitial bursa (arrow) arising from irritation
between the scapula and rib 6.

Figure 6.13

Position to facilitate examination of levator
scapulae.

Scapulothoracic bursal involvement

Bursal inflammatory changes can occur either
at the junction of the scapula with the costal
surface of rib six, or at the superior vertebral
border of the scapula.

An adventitial bursa can form at the junction of the inferior–distal surface of the scapula with the sixth rib, which leads to pain
during the throwing act. Treatment consists
of rest, the use of nonsteroidal anti-
inflammatory agents and, at times, an injection into the tender, swollen bursal area. If
this fails, surgical excision of the bursa is
indicated, with excellent results to be
expected (*Figure 6.12*).

Levator scapulae syndromes are rare and
often misdiagnosed entities. Estwanik (1989)
reviewed the records of 66 patients who had
been treated for levator scapulae syndrome.
Although the syndrome occurs frequently and
is well documented, it often goes un-
recognized due to a lack of awareness of the
condition. The diagnosis can be facilitated by
positioning the patient so that the scapula is
elevated, thus making the levator muscle insertion protrude. This area on palpation will
be painful. This syndrome is also known as a
superior scapular syndrome, a scapulocostal
syndrome, or a scapulothoracic bursitis.

The levator scapula muscle elevates the
scapula while rotating the glenoid cavity
downward; it also helps to turn the cervical
spine. Degeneration of the tendon can be
expected to occur in or near the insertion of
the levator scapular tendon. It arises from the
transverse process from cervical vertebra C1
through C4 and has a broad insertion into the
superior medial border of the scapula. Overhead activities in sports involving repetitive
shoulder motion can cause tendonitis of the
levator scapula muscle. To facilitate examination of the levator scapula syndrome, the
patient should be prone with the shoulders
abducted (*Figure 6.13*). This position allows

for prominence of the scapula, thus exposing the superior medial border, the site of the levator insertion. Treatment of this syndrome consists of physical therapy and/or local injection of an anesthetic. Forms of physical therapy include spray-and-stretch, ice massage, phonophoresis, or iontophoresis with a corticosteroid, high-voltage galvanic stimulation, stretching exercise, transverse friction massage and manual trigger-point therapy. Posture awareness and strengthening programs should be instituted.

Diagnosis of this condition is difficult to make since it can be confused with many disorders relating to the neck, shoulder and upper back, such as lower disc attrition with radiculopathy, cervical arthritis, cervical strain, fibromyalgia syndrome or myofascial pain syndrome, suprascapular nerve entrapment, symptomatology of gallbladder problems, angina, and lung tumor.

McKenzie exercise program, and other modalities. At times, trigger-point injections are indicated and can be extremely helpful. If an area of muscle spasm that recreates the pain can be located, it is advantageous to inject a local anesthetic, with or without the use of an injectable steroid. If pain persists and is worse at night, a lung tumor with metastatic disease to the cervical spine should be ruled out (*Figure 6.14*).

Brachial plexus stretch syndromes

Brachial plexus stretch syndromes have been described previously and are discussed more fully in subsequent chapters.

Extrinsic causes of pain in and about the shoulder

Arthritis and/or tumors of the cervical spine are causes of shoulder girdle pain, particularly in those beyond the age of 35. At present, there are many older people active not only in professional sports, but also in recreational sports. Arthritis is heralded by neck and shoulder pain. There are trigger points in the supraspinatus, infraspinatus, rhomboids, and scalene musculature. Shoulder girdle function is usually normal; however, pain can result in a decrease in shoulder girdle function and eventually an adhesive capsulitis will occur. It is very difficult to decipher which came first, that is, the cervical problem or the shoulder problem, so treatment must be directed towards both areas. The treatment of cervical spine involvement consists of cervical traction, spray and stretch techniques,

Peripheral nerve involvement about the shoulder girdle

The suprascapular nerve arises from the upper trunk of the brachial plexus at the confluence of C5 and C6, and derives most of its fibers from C5. It is the only branch of the upper trunk that is directed posteriorly and laterally beneath the trapezius to the upper border of the scapula. It innervates the supraspinatus and infraspinatus musculature and is predisposed to compression, irritation, or traction of the nerve, either from forceful depression of the shoulder or with certain repetitive abnormal movements as in posterior shoulder subluxation.

The condition can be confused with rotator cuff lesions and this must be taken into consideration in order to treat it properly. Diagnosis and treatment of the problem are discussed in more detail in subsequent chapters.

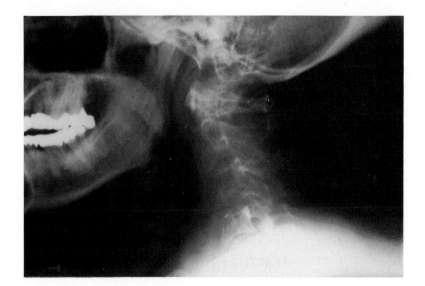

Figure 6.14

Radiograph demonstrating
metastatic disease of the
cervical spine.

Pain of the deep, relentless type is associated with weakness of forward flexion and external rotation of the humerus when the entrapment is at the notch. If the nerve is trapped distal to the branch to the supraspinatus, pain occurs in association with external rotation weakness, although not with weakness of flexion in the scapular plane. Atrophy of the infraspinatus muscle, however, is evident without atrophy of the supraspinatus in this instance. EMG/NCV (nerve-conduction velocity) study may help to establish where the nerve is trapped. Exploration of the nerve may be necessary once the diagnosis has been made. If the lesion is at the notch, careful dissection through the trapezius must be performed, the suprascapular artery ligated, and the transverse scapular ligament transected to free the nerve. If the entrapped area is distal to the notch, the supraspinatus muscle must be elevated from the fossa in order to find the entrapped area of the nerve.

Recently during surgery, we demonstrated involvement of the suprascapular nerve distal to its penetration into the supraspinatus muscle with a ganglion cyst. A resection of the cyst effected relief of the pain with eventual improvement, not only of the muscle atrophy of the infraspinatus, but also with EMG improvement (*Figure 6.15*). Compression from malunited or ununited clavicular fractures may also affect the suprascapular nerve in its most proximal portion.

Musculocutaneous nerve injury

Musculocutaneous nerve injury is discussed in Chapter 12.

DATE **12/15/88**

NERVE CONDUCTION STUDY:

NERVE	LATENCY (MS.)		DISTANCE (CM.)		AMPLITUDE (MV)		VELOCITY (M/S)	
	R	L	R	L	R	L	R	L
MOTOR								
MEDIAN								
WRIST	3.6		5		11			
ANTEC. FOSSA	8.6		27		10		59	
Erb to delto	3.8		17		needle			
infras	4.0	2.4	18	18	needle	needle		
supras	3.6	2.2	12	16	needle	needle		
SENSORY								
MEDIAN	2.5		13.5		55		54	
ULNAR	2.5		13.5		30		54	
F wave(APB)	29.0	29.2						

ELECTROMYOGRAPHY STUDY:

MUSCLE	INSERTIONAL ACTIVITY		FIBS/POS. WAVES		FASICU-LATIONS		.....MOTOR UNITS.....	
	R	L	R	L	R	L	R	L
ABDUC. POL. BR.	nl		0		0		nl	
1ST DORSAL INTEROS.	nl		0		0		nl	
BRACHIORAD.	nl		0		0		nl	
BICEPS	nl		0		0		nl	
TRICEPS	nl		0		0		nl	
DELTOID	nl		0		0		nl	
Supraspin	inc	nl	4+	0	0	0	one unit inc dur, poly	
Infraspin	inc	nl	4+	0	0	0	one unit inc dur	
Paraspinal								
C4-5	nl		0		0		nl	
C5-6	nl		0		0		nl	
C6-7	nl		0		0		nl	
C7-8	nl		0		0		nl	

Interpretation: 1). The nerve conduction velocity shows prolonged latency
Erb to spinati on right.
2). The EMG shows denervation changes right supra and
infraspinatus.

Conclusion: right suprascapular neuropathy

(a)

Figure 6.15

(a, b, c) Representative EMG studies of the
suprascapular nerve-entrapment phenomenon.

Figure 6.15 (cont'd)

DATE 9/21/89

NERVE CONDUCTION STUDY:

NERVE	LATENCY (MS.)		DISTANCE (CM.)		AMPLITUDE (MV)		VELOCITY (M/S)	
	R	L	R	L	R	L	R	L
MOTOR								
MEDIAN								
WRIST								
ANTEC. FOSSA								
ERB to								
infras	4.6	2.2	17	17	needle	needle		
supras	5.0	2.0	11	11	needle	needle		

SENSORY
  MEDIAN
  ULNAR

ELECTROMYOGRAPHY STUDY:

MUSCLE	INSERTIONAL ACTIVITY		FIBS/POS. WAVES		FASICU-LATIONS		.........MOTOR UNITS.........	
	R	L	R	L	R	L	R	L
Suprasp	nl	nl	0	0	0	0	mod dec # inc dur exc poly/	
Infraspin	nl	nl	0	0	0	0	mod dec # inc dur exc poly/	

Interpretation: 1) the nerve conduction velocity shows prolonged right
                   suprascap nerve latencies.
                2) the EMG shows chronic partial denervation right supras
                   and infraspinatus

Conclusion: right suprascapular neuropathy. Compared to the pre op study of
            12/15/88 there has been marked improvement in the EMG but
            further prolongation in the motor latencies.

(b)

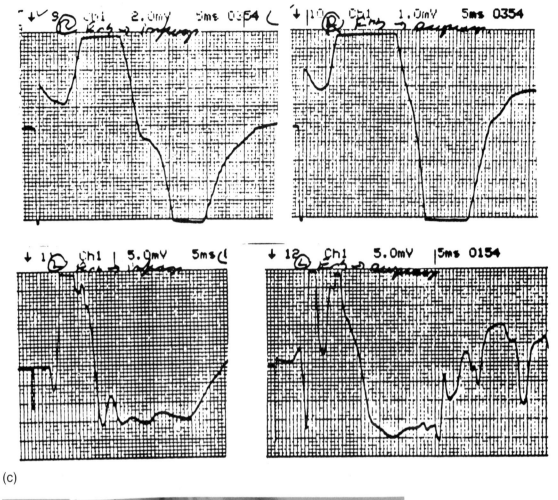

(c)

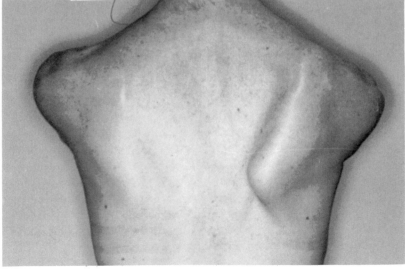

Figure 6.16

Winging of the scapula due to serratus anterior paralysis caused by back packing.

Axillary nerve involvement

The axillary nerve can be trapped in the quadrangular space by a fascial sling or hypertrophied muscle, causing pain in the shoulder girdle. The condition is most often treated by avoidance of shoulder overactivity and a remedial exercise program. If this fails, the nerve in the quadrangular space could be surgically decompressed.

Back pack palsy

A compression syndrome affecting nerves about the shoulder has been reported to occur in back packers. The commonly involved peripheral nerves include the spinal accessory nerve, suprascapular nerve, and the long thoracic nerve. There are complaints of weakness of the arm and shoulder without obvious injury. Atrophy about the shoulder girdle is noted, along with winging of the scapula (*Figure 6.16*). Electrodiagnostic studies should be performed to confirm the diagnosis. Viral neuropathies or the plexopathy of Turner and Parsonage should be ruled out. Treatment consists of modifying the back pack-carrying technique, in association with a rehabilitative program. The prognosis is good with over 90 percent recovery rate within three months if treatment guidelines are followed and maintained.

Neurovascular syndromes

The thoracic outlet syndrome has caused symptoms in baseball players and javelin throwers. The diagnosis is difficult to make because the findings are similar to the signs of rotator cuff pathology, shoulder subluxation, or brachial plexus stretch injury. Arterial occlusion has been reported to occur due to pressure on the artery by the pectoralis minor tendon. Venous occlusions have occurred, albeit rarely, during the hyperabduction cocking phase of the throwing motion in baseball players, in the axillary and subclavian veins.

Incidence of shoulder injuries in specific sports

Basketball

Injuries to the shoulder comprise only 3 percent of all injuries in professional basketball players. Of these injuries, 88 percent were contusions and muscle strains. Although overuse injuries in the shoulder have recently been reported, they are not as common as in baseball or other throwing sports. Hyperextension of the arm during a lay-up in association with abduction and external rotation can predispose a shoulder to anterior subluxation or dislocation.

Dance

Klemp and Learmonth (1984) reported that 3 out of 114 injuries sustained by professional ballet dancers involved the shoulder. Zarins and Rowe (1984) reported a case of chronic pain in the scapulothoracic joint from isolated shoulder motions utilized in dance; however, the author has never seen a chronic overuse problem develop in and about the shoulder girdle in dancers.

Diving

Competitive divers are prone to two types of shoulder injuries, both caused by improper water entry. The flat entry has been implicated in anterior shoulder subluxation or rotator cuff injury. These injuries usually occur in young divers who have inadequate shoulder strength. Anterior glenohumeral dislocation is another injury that occurs with diving; however, it is unusual, and when it occurs, does so at water entry as the result of the diver not clasping the hands prior to entry.

Football

The shoulder is the point of impact in most tackle and blocking plays so it is not surprising that the shoulder girdle is frequently injured in football. The frequency of shoulder injury in football was found to be second only to the knee according to Shields and Zomar (1982).

The most common shoulder injuries in football are contusions, acromioclavicular joint injuries, brachial plexus injuries, rotator cuff tears, muscle strains, glenohumeral instability, and clavicle fractures.

In a study of 164 acromioclavicular joint injuries in athletes, Cox (1981) reported 41 percent to occur in football, while wrestling and lacrosse were next in frequency in occurrence.

Golf

The golf swing, according to Pink, Jobe, and Perry (1990) is broken down into five segments:

1   Take away: from ball address to the end of the backswing.

2   Forward swing: from the end of the backswing until the club is horizontal.

3   Acceleration: from horizontal club to ball contact.

4   Early follow through: from ball contact to horizontal club.

5   Late follow through: from horizontal club to the end of motion.

They concluded that the infraspinatus and supraspinatus acted in concert as external rotators, abductors, and stabilizers of the shoulder. The subscapularis is most active at acceleration when the arm is internally rotating. The latissimus dorsi and pectoralis major are the power-driving muscles of the shoulder, with the latissimus responding before the pectoralis. The pectoralis contributes the most activity of all the muscles tested since it assists the rotation and forceful adduction of the arm. The anterior deltoid is most active since it lifts and flexes the arm, whereas the other two heads of the deltoid are relatively noncontributory to the golf swing.

Most injuries occur during the impact phase when the golfer strikes the ball.

Excessive muscle strength is not required to play golf although strengthening and conditioning programs are important. Excessive or improper weightlifting or resistance training can cause muscles to tighten with loss of the appropriate rhythm and co-ordination of the arm. Shoulder impingement syndrom has been reported to occur frequently from golf, and rotator cuff tears are not uncommon in the golfer.

Gymnastics

Snook (1979), in a study of 71 women gymnasts, reported 66 major shoulder injuries, 45 of which were traumatic in onset and 21 repetitive. It appears that experienced gymnasts are likely to experience stress failure and inexperienced gymnasts are more likely to sustain acute injury. The experienced gymnasts' shoulder frequently demonstrates acromioclavicular degenerative changes and osteochondral bodies of the glenohumeral joint.

Ice hockey

Prior to the use of face masks, injuries to the head, scalp, face, and eye were reported in more than 50 percent of all injuries sustained in ice hockey. Since the use of helmets and face masks is mandatory in amateur hockey in the USA, and are employed more often in professional hockey, the frequency of these injuries has decreased.

The upper extremity is involved in approximately 20 percent of total hockey injuries. The percentage of injuries that involve the shoulder is reported to be between 8 and 22 percent. Overuse injuries are uncommon since the arm is seldom used in the overhead position.

The most common shoulder injuries are the acromioclavicular separation, anterior dislocation or subluxation of the shoulder, contusions, brachial plexus injuries and traumatic osteolysis of the distal clavicle.

Norfray et al. (1977) found that 46 percent of professional ice hockey players had radiographic abnormalities of the clavicle. Acromioclavicular joint injuries were found to be most common in professional players whereas acute clavicle fracture injuries were most common in amateur players. Post-traumatic changes of the distal end of the clavicle were frequently seen in the amateur player; however, these changes were also noted in the professional player. Changes about the acromioclavicular joint included widening of the joint, ununited clavicle fractures, exuberant callous, and distal clavicular osteolysis.

Hovelius (1978) reported an 8 percent incidence of primary glenohumeral dislocation in hockey players. More than 90 percent of players over 20 years of age had recurrence of their dislocation.

Of interest, one third of the players who had recurrent shoulder instability not treated by surgery were able to continue playing ice hockey.

As stated previously, traumatic osteolysis of the distal end of the clavicle has been reported following acute traumatic injuries in sports including hockey. Cahill (1983) demonstrated that 45 of 46 men with osteolysis of the clavicle lifted weights as part of their physical condition. **This suggests that repetitive weightlifting by hockey players is more likely to cause the condition than is traumatic injury**.

Martial arts

Shoulders are involved in 7 percent of all injuries of martial arts. The injuries that occurred most commonly were contusions, sprains, dislocations, and fractures, in descending order of frequency. Of all injuries in Judo 44 percent involved the shoulder. In Aikido, the shoulder roll is used frequently and acromioclavicular separations are commonly seen. Karate has been reported to be an infrequent cause of shoulder pain; however, the author has seen a number of overuse injuries to the shoulder from karate. The apparent reason for these overuse injuries is the fact that deceleration of the upper limb without an object is more rapid than the throwing motion if an object such as a ball *is* thrown. The injuries seen included a stress fracture of the coracoid, a brachial plexus stretch traction injury, anterior shoulder subluxation, posterior shoulder subluxation, and rotator cuff tears.

Back packing

The brachial plexus is affected in carrying a back pack. Normally, the peripheral nerves involved include the spinal accessory nerve, the suprascapular nerve, and the long thoracic nerve. Atrophy of the shoulder girdle and arm is seen, as well as winging of the scapula.

Viral neuropathies may mimic back pack palsy and should be ruled out.

Treatment consists of the patient modifying or eliminating the back pack as the source of nerve compression, in association with a remedial exercise program. During recovery, it is important to avoid further trauma to the brachial plexus. Prognosis is good with almost 90 percent recovery rate within three months if proper treatment guidelines are followed.

Racket sports

Shoulder injuries have been reported to account for approximately 5 percent of all injuries incurred while playing racket sports. The acromioclavicular joint is a common site of injury because of impact of the shoulder against a wall. Since overhead motions are not frequently used in racquet ball or squash, chronic shoulder overuse syndromes are uncommon.

Snow skiing — alpine

Approximately 20 percent of all downhill ski injuries involve the shoulder. The shoulder is the second most common site of upper extremity injury, the thumb being the most common. The most usual types of shoulder injuries in skiing are glenohumeral dislocation, greater tuberosity fracture, acromioclavicular separation, clavicular fracture, humeral shaft fracture, scapula fracture, and rotator cuff injuries. Glenohumeral dislocations comprise approximately 10 percent of upper extremity injuries in skiing. Morgan and Davis (1982) postulate that the ski pole is often responsible for the dislocation since the ski-pole basket can catch on vegetation, thereby extending the arm and dislocating the shoulder, or the pole can be planted during a fall forward, forcing the shoulder into abduction and external rotation.

Swimming

Chronic shoulder pain is the most common musculoskeletal problem in competitive swimmers. 'Swimmer's shoulder' as coined by Kennedy and Hawkins (1974) is used to describe the chronic overuse syndrome of the shoulder that occurs in approximately 3 percent of long-distance swimmers. Adams (1968) reported an incidence of shoulder pain in 10 percent of competitive swimmers between the ages of 11 and 12. Fowler (1983) and Richardson et al (1980) state the incidence of shoulder pain in highly competitive swimmers to be as high as 50 percent. Richardson found that 92 percent of competitive swimmers with shoulder pain swam either freestyle, backstroke or butterfly since they use very similar motions of adduction, internal rotation, abduction, and external rotation. Problems encountered were subacromial impingement, anterior subluxation, and posterior subluxation. A subacromial impingement syndrome occurs in the freestyle and butterfly strokes since they use the motions of throwing sports. Anterior subluxation is most common in backstrokers. Fowler found 54 percent of competitive swimmers examined had posterior humeral subluxation. However, a controlled group of non-swimming athletes of similar age had a 52 percent incidence of posterior instability, which may be physiologic in the active swimming athlete.

Tennis

Acromial impingement symptoms are common in tennis players. The tennis serve is basically the same motion as in throwing sports. Rotator cuff tears are not that uncommon in tennis players, increasing in frequency as the player ages.

Weightlifting

The common injuries about the shoulder incurred with weightlifting are subacromial impingement, rotator cuff pathology, distal clavicle arthritis and osteolysis, glenohumeral subluxation, pectoralis major rupture, and secondary bicipital tendinitis.

Wrestling

Shoulder injuries account for 16 percent of all wrestling injuries. In fact, the shoulder is the second most common injury, with the knee being the most common area. Acromioclavicular, sternoclavicular, and glenohumeral dislocations are the most common injuries.

Water polo

Water polo has a high incidence of shoulder injury. An incidence of 36 percent of rotator cuff tendinitis, with a significant involvement of the acromioclavicular joint on a degenerative basis, has been reported (Rowe, 1988, p. 430). This is an alarming incidence of impingement-type problems and most probably is due to poor training techniques both in swimming and throwing.

Volleyball

The constant use of the upper extremities in volleyball, associated with the force generated in slamming of the ball towards the opponent, commonly causes soft-tissue and bone lesions about the shoulder. These include the impingement syndrome, osteolysis of the acromioclavicular joint, and rotator cuff strains including tears, strains, and tearing of the pectoralis major, teres major, and latissimus dorsi musculature. There have been reports of glenoid/ labral tearing in volleyball with the secondary occurrence of bicipital tendinitis.

Bracker et al (1990) described shoulder pain in a 14-year-old volleyball player with chronic pain in the overhead position. Radiography and MRI revealed multiple calcifications involving the shoulder joint and the biceps tendon sheath. Surgical removal of these calcifications improved the condition. Surgical chondromatosis is rare, particularly in the shoulder; it is more common in the knee and hip. The disease is usually monoarticular.

7

The sternoclavicular joint

Injuries to this joint are rare as noted not only by the author but by others such as Rowe (1958) and Rockwood and Green (1984). Atraumatic dislocations have been reported by Booth and Roper (1979). Acute, traumatic anterior dislocation, the most common, may be treated with benign neglect. Posterior dislocations should be reduced either by closed or open methods and are true medical emergencies.

Anatomy

The sternoclavicular joint is the sole articulation between the upper extremity and the axial skeleton through the clavicle. It would be an unstable joint, if it were not for its strong ligaments. The sternoclavicular ligaments are on the anterior and posterior aspects of the joint, while the interclavicular ligament supports the superior surface. The costoclavicular ligament supports the inferior aspect of the joint between the clavicle and the first rib. Functional range of motion is 35° of elevation

and 45° of rotation. The major concern with regard to injuries to the sternoclavicular joint is the vital structures that lie beneath it (*Figure 7.1*).

Mechanism of injury

Injury to the sternoclavicular joint results from a blow transmitted to the point of the shoulder or from a direct blow to the clavicle or chest with the shoulder in extension. When the point of the shoulder is struck, this would predispose to an anterior dislocation. A blow to the anterior chest or clavicle usually predisposes to a posterior dislocation.

Types of injuries

Various types of injury to the sternoclavicular joint occur (Table 7.1).

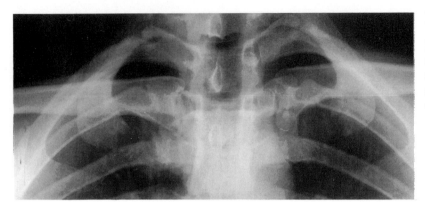

Figure 7.1

Radiographic study demonstrating overlapping structures about the sternoclavicular joint.

Table 7.1

Injuries to the sternoclavicular joint.

Traumatic
Sprains
   Grade I — no displacement
   Grade II — partial subluxation with
   rupture of the sternoclavicular ligament,
   but without rupture of the costoclavicular
   ligament
   Grade III — complete dislocation either
   anterior or posterior

Nontraumatic
Voluntary
Luxation and/or dislocation without trauma

Diagnosis

A history of a blow to the shoulder or direct blow to the chest or clavicle with resultant pain in the sternal area is usually recorded. Initially, soft-tissue swelling occurs and may conceal an anterior dislocation. A posterior dislocation is difficult to recognize but usually the patient complains of extreme discomfort and has a shortened forequarter.

Diagnostic aids

The area is difficult to interpret on X-ray since there is overlapping of the rib, the sternum, and the clavicle at the joint. Oblique views and tomography are helpful. Computed tomography scans have proven to be successful and should always be taken if a question arises regarding a possible dislocation (*Figure 7.2*). If pain persists without evidence of dislocation, a bone scan is indicated in an effort to rule out synovitis and/or a fracture (*Figure 7.3*). Rockwood and Green (1984) state that use of an X-ray tube tilted at 40° from the vertical and aimed directly at the manubrium is helpful.

Treatment for subluxation

With Grade I and Grade II injuries, conservative measures consist of ice, a sling if necessary, and anti-inflammatory agents as needed. Usually, by the second or third week, most of the pain has subsided and a gradual return to function is indicated.

Dislocation

Anterior

If an anterior dislocation is seen early there is a good chance of a manipulative reduction. This can be carried out under intravenous medication. A roll is placed between the shoulder blades, and the clavicle is reduced by manual assistance. A figure-of-eight dressing or plaster immobilization can be used. The

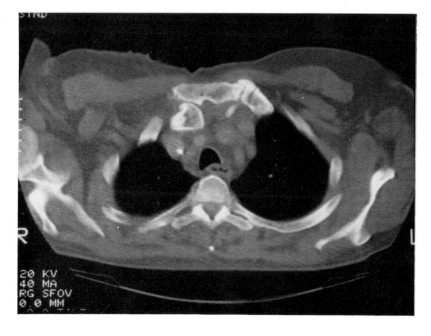

Figure 7.2

CT scan of posterior sternoclavicular joint dislocation.

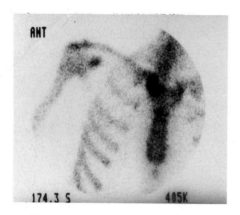 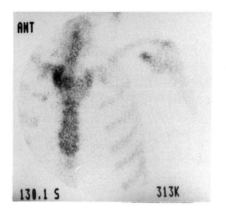

Figure 7.3

Bone scan of sternoclavicular joints demonstrating increased isotope uptake in the right sternoclavicular joint.

author prefers plaster immobilization (*Figure 7.4*). Complete elevation and extension of the arm should be avoided for three weeks. If reduction is incomplete or cannot be accomplished, it has been found that the majority of anterior dislocations will do well without any further attempt at reduction.

Posterior

Closed manipulation is recommended for a posterior dislocation, followed by open methods if the reduction fails. A sandbag is placed between the scapula, with traction applied to the abducted and extended arm. This technique is reported to be successful in the majority of cases. If reduction fails or if the patient is having difficulty breathing, open reduction is necessary. A vascular surgeon and blood should be available, if surgery is indicated. A subperiosteal dissection is the safest way to expose the clavicle, followed by traction being applied to the arm by an assistant or by a towel clip grasping the clavicle. Pin fixation is necessary, hence a threaded pin of adequate strength should be used. The patient should be instructed in feeling for the pin every day since pins have a tendency to migrate. A modified plaster device as previously described for anterior dislocations is also utilized. The pin is removed within 5–6 weeks. Isometric exercises for the involved extremity are suggested until pin removal. Following removal of the pin and immobilization a range of motion is begun in conjunction with a remedial exercise program.

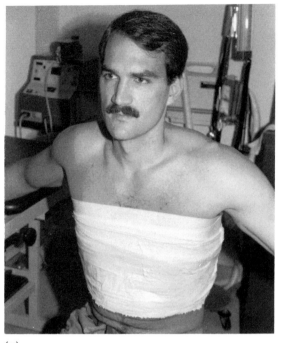

(a)

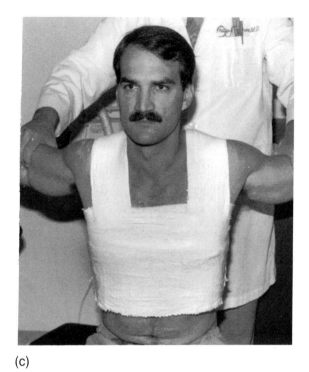

(c)

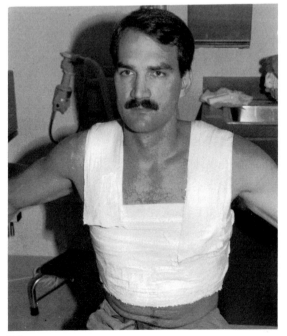

(b)

Figure 7.4

Plaster immobilization technique.

8
The clavicle

Anatomical considerations

The clavicle has an S-shape wherein the straight middle third connects to the outer and medial thirds of the clavicle: this area is particularly important to understand when intramedullary fixation is used. The clavicle is well supplied with blood through its muscle attachments, therefore accounting for its marked ability to heal. The fact that the subclavian and axillary vessels and the nerves of the brachial plexus lie directly beneath the middle third of the clavicle is of importance.

Injuries

Fractures most commonly occur in the middle third, thus accounting for approximately 80 percent of all clavicle fractures. Of these, 44 percent occur at the junction of the middle and outer thirds (*Figure 8.1*).

Diagnosis

The patient gives a history of falling in the area of the shoulder or being struck directly on the clavicle, experiencing immediate pain and inability to raise the arm.

Radiographic examination should be carried out as quickly as possible. A film which does not show the entire clavicle including the shoulder girdle, the upper third of the humerus, and the sternal end of the clavicle should never be accepted.

Treatment of middle-third fractures

The majority of middle-third clavicular fractures respond to closed treatment. The incidence of nonunion following closed treatment is extremely low, with reports varying from 0.1 to 0.8 percent in a large series. If open treatment is entertained, the nonunion rate increases fourfold. A closed reduction is effected by elevating the arms and shoulders and then extending them. Immobilization is accomplished by slings, figure-of-eight dressings, or plaster immobilization. The author's preference is plaster immobilization as demonstrated (see *Figure 7.4*). This is especially so in adults with an unstable displaced comminuted fracture. Figure-of-eight dressings can be dangerous since they can

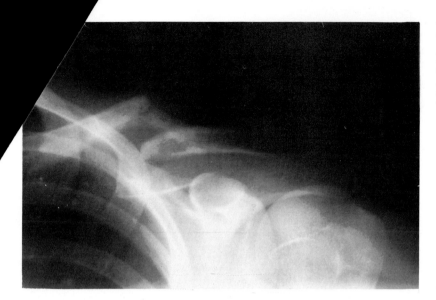

Figure 8.1

Fractured clavicle (a) 6 weeks and (b) 11 months post trauma.

(a)

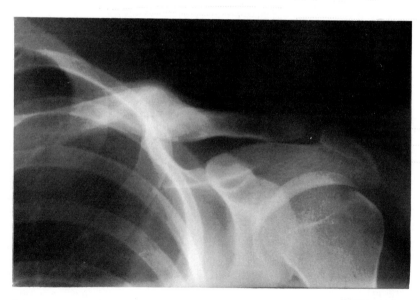

(b)

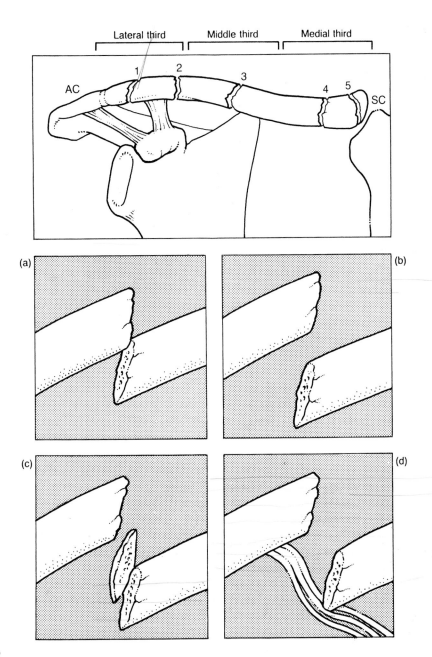

Figure 8.2

Clavicle fractures: the classification of Thompson
(1990, p. 14). AC, acromioclavicular joint; SC,
sternoclavicular joint; 1–5, locations. Locations
are shown as 1–5; displacements are shown as (a)
less than 100 percent, (b, c) greater than 100
percent, and (d) neurovascular compromise.

increase deformity if not properly applied. They also can cause distal extremity with numbness and tingling in the hand.

Immobilization is usually discontinued after 3–4 weeks. Rehabilitation is started immediately upon disappearance of most of the pain, with the use of isometric exercises for the extremities. Following the removal of the device, a more intensive program is started since motion can be allowed to progress. Strengthening programs should be encouraged and are outlined in Chapter 14.

Fractures of the outer third of the clavicle

Neer (1968) states there are two types of fractures, type I and type II. Type I fractures are stable since the coracoclavicular ligaments are attached to both fracture fragments, therefore these fractures will heal promptly. In type II injuries, the coracoclavicular ligaments remain remain attached to the distal fragment and are detached from the medial fragment, thus allowing upper displacement of the proximal medial fragment. It is very difficult to eliminate motion with closed treatment, and therefore, the rate of nonunion is higher. This fracture should be reduced and transfixed with fixation of choice. Appropriately applied threaded pins of sufficient strength are, however, usually adequate to maintain reduction.

Complications of clavicular fracture

Thompson (1990) classified clavicle fractures from 1 through 5 (*Figure 8.2*). Type IIIb fractures (completely displaced fractures of the middle third) account for 90 percent of nonunions of the clavicle in adults and about 3 percent of all clavicle fractures in the adult. Thompson states that the type IIIb clavicle fracture should be considered for primary ORIF if it cannot be converted to a type IIIa with bony contact.

Jupiter (1989) suggested non-union of a clavicular fracture, while an uncommon occurrence, is a difficult management problem since pain at the non-union site can lead to significant functional impairment of the involved limb, particularly in the athlete. Associated clavicular deformity has the potential to compromise the subclavian muscles, vessels, or brachial plexus.

The predisposing factors contributing to clavicular nonunion include open fractures, re-fracture, associated polytrauma, instability, duration of immobilization, and initial fracture displacement. Rowe (1968) noted that the commonly used figure-of-eight clavicle strap, if improperly applied, may add to the downward displacement of the lateral fragment in the middle third of a type IIIb fracture. This is another reason for using a plaster dressing.

When nonunion occurs, plate fixation is the treatment of choice, since efficient skeletal fixation must be performed.

9

The acromioclavicular joint

Anatomical features

The acromioclavicular joint is an important part of the functional mechanics of the shoulder girdle. This joint, together with the sternoclavicular joint, contributes 60° to the total 180° of abduction of the arm. It also participates in protraction and retraction of the shoulder. The size and shape of the articular surfaces of the joint provide no stability, yet the arrangement of the ligaments are such that it is very stable.

The joint is formed by the flat medial margin of the acromion and the distal end of the clavicle. These are enveloped in a weak relaxed capsule. The capsule is reinforced above by the strong superior acromioclavicular ligament and below by the weaker inferior acromioclavicular ligament.

Superiorly, the tendinous fibers of the origin of the deltoid and trapezius span the joint and blend with the superior ligament. The coracoclavicular ligaments span the interval between the clavicle and coracoid process: they are comprised of two bundles, the trapezoid and the conoid ligaments. The acromioclavicular ligaments contribute approxi-mately two-thirds of the constraining force to superior and posterior displacement; however, with greater displacement the cora-coclavicular ligaments contribute the major share of constraint.

Biomechanical features

Fukuda et al (1986) in a biomechanical study of the ligamentous system of the acromioclavicular joint noted several points: the acromioclavicular ligament acts as a primary constraint for posterior displacement of the clavicle and of posterior axial rotation; the conoid ligament appears to be more important than previously described in that it plays a primary role in constraining anterior and superior rotation as well as anterior and superior displacement of the clavicle; and the trapezoid ligament contributes less constraint to movement of the clavicle in both the horizontal and vertical plane (the exception is when clavicular movement and axial compression are towards the acromion process).

Clinical relevance

All of the ligaments that support the acromio-clavicular joint provide a substantial contribution to its stability. The contribution changes with direction and the amount of loading. If maximum strength of healing after injury is the goal, all ligaments should be allowed to participate in the healing process. Some repair methods, notably those involving excision of the distal end of the clavicle, may not make this possible. When the anterior part of the acromioclavicular ligament and capsule is divided, joint subluxation of approximately 50 percent occurs. When the entire capsule, the acromioclavicular ligament, and the trapezius and deltoid muscle attachments are divided, the clavicle could be completely dislocated posteriorly but could be subluxed only superiorly. When the trapezoid ligament is also divided, upward dislocation occurs and when the conoid ligament is divided instead of the trapezoid ligament, upward dislocation occurs to a slightly greater degree.

Urist (1946) concluded that injury to the acromioclavicular capsule, ligament and supporting muscles was necessary to allow subluxation or dislocation posteriorly and that further injury involving the coracoclavicular ligaments would allow greater displacement, particularly in a superior direction. Fukuda et al (1986) determined that the most common directions of pathologic displacement of the clavicle that are seen clinically are superior and posterior. With lesser amounts of displacement and induced load, the acromioclavicular ligament contributed approximately two-thirds of the constraining force to superior displacement. With a larger displacement and induced load, the conoid ligament contributed the major share. In the direction of posterior displacement of the clavicle, the acromioclavicular ligament contributed approximately 90 percent of the ligamentous constraint at either lesser or greater amounts of loading and displacement. The studies of Fukuda et al and Urist emphasized the importance of the acromioclavicular ligament and its contribution to stability between the clavicle and the scapula.

Mechanisms of injury

Injuries to the capsule and ligament of the acromioclavicular joint usually occur as the result of a direct downward blow to the tip of the shoulder wherein the arm is usually at the side and adducted. The resultant force produces varying types of sprains depending upon the amount of force incurred at the time of injury. Sprains occur and vary from grade I through to grade VI (*Figure 9.1*).

Clinical diagnosis

Pain, the predominant feature, is at the top of the shoulder. Motion about the shoulder is lost; the degree varies with the grade of the sprain. For instance, in a grade I sprain, shoulder motion is complete but slow and painful at the extremes whereas, in a grade III sprain, there is no motion at the shoulder because of the pain. Grade III sprains are clearly visible in that the clavicle is dislocated superiorly (*Figure 9.2*). A posterior clavicular dislocation is difficult to identify due to the absence of a deformity superiorly. On close examination, there is a palpable prominence of the end of the clavicle posterior to the acromion.

Diagnostic aids

Radiographic examination will be normal in grade I and most grade II sprains. In grade III sprains however, the clavicle is superior in

Figure 9.1

Grades of sprains of acromioclavicular joint.
(Courtesy of Cook and Heiner, 1990, pp. 511–12.)

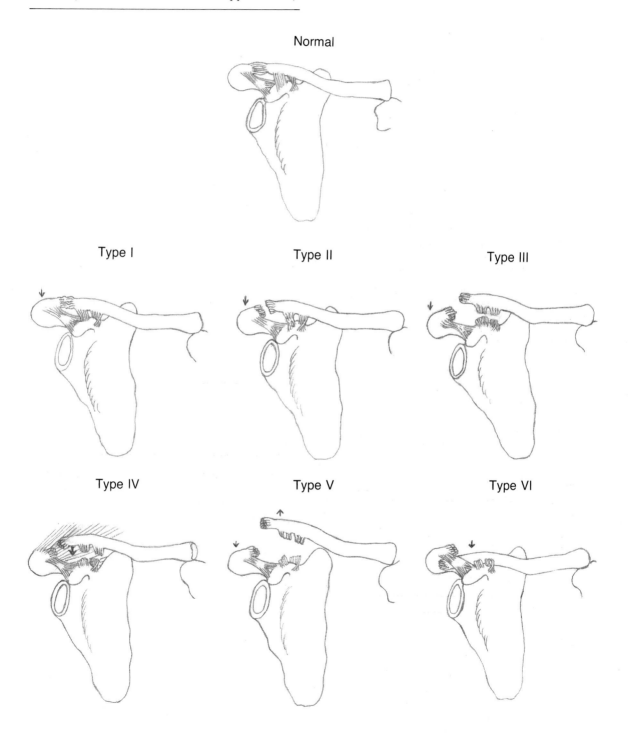

Normal

Type I

Type II

Type III

Type IV

Type V

Type VI

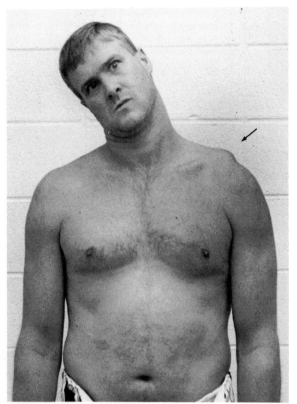

Figure 9.2

A grade III sprain, visible as the clavicle is dislocated superiorly.

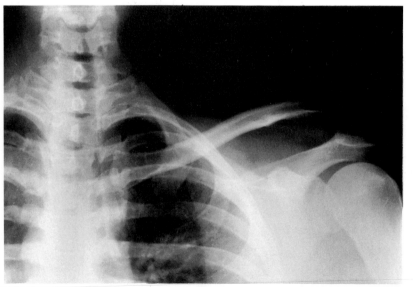

Figure 9.3

In grade III sprains, the clavicle is dislocated superiorly in most instances.

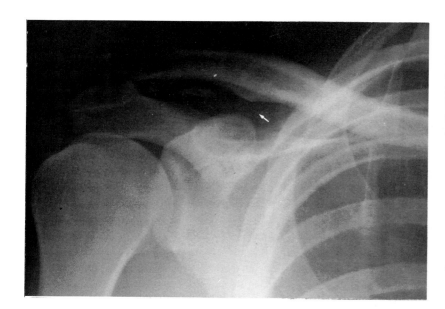

Figure 9.4

Radiograph of posterior dislocation, showing narrowing of the space between the clavicle and the coracoid (arrow).

most instances (*Figure 9.3*), and in the rare form of posterior dislocation, the AP radiograph shows narrowing of the space between the undersurface of the clavicle and coracoid rather than an increased space (*Figure 9.4*). Both shoulders should be visualized on the same film, if possible. If a question persists regarding a posterior dislocation, a true axillary view or a CT scan will reveal this problem.

injuries may develop late traumatic joint changes and will need a resection of the distal end of the clavicle for pain relief. It is important to note that after a resection of the distal end of the clavicle, particularly in a throwing athlete, there may be formation of heterotopic bone on the undersurface of the clavicle which can cause a painful syndrome which in essence is an impingement (*Figure 9.5*).

Treatment

Grade I and II injuries

Injuries of grades I and II are treated conservatively with ice packs, a sling, and anti-inflammatory agents. The pain usually subsides within ten days; however, it may last longer. The sport and the position played determines when a player can return to a sporting activity. A soccer or football player, who does not have to elevate his arm, can return sooner than the tennis player, swimmer, or baseball player. Some grade II

Grade III injuries

Some clinicians do not attempt to reduce dislocation and stabilize it. They utilize a sling for comfort, not for reduction, and within 3–6 weeks allow activity as tolerated.

Hawkins (1980) and Imatani et al (1975) compared operative versus nonoperative treatment, and concluded that the nonoperative treatment yielded results as good as, if not better than, surgical treatment.

MacDonald et al (1988) stated that 'when comparing surgical and conservative treatment programs for function following complete acromioclavicular separation, the non-

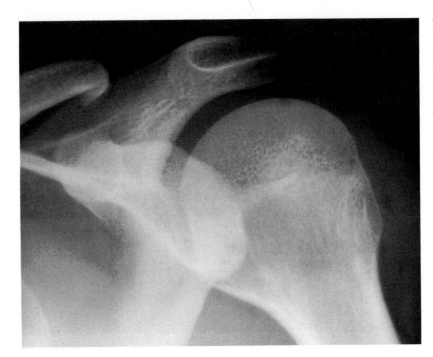

Figure 9.5

Heterotopic bone
formation on undersurface
of clavicle following
resection of distal clavicle.

surgical treatment is superior in restoring
normal shoulder function within the first year
following injury'. The majority of strength and
flexibility tests revealed no significant difference between the nonsurgical and surgical
groups. The nonsurgical group was statis-
tically superior to the surgical group in eccentric abduction (fast speeds), concentric external
rotation (slow speeds), eccentric external rotation (fast speeds), eccentric abduction (slow
speeds), and flexibility in external rotation.

Welsh et al (1985), after determining
shoulder strength following acromioclavicular injury, stated that grade II injuries treated
conservatively had the most pain and stiffness
despite their strong shoulders. Patients with
grade III injuries who were treated operatively
related their overall outcome below that of
those treated conservatively. Welsh concluded that, from the standpoint of objective
strength, nonsurgical treatment of grade III

acromioclavicular injury is as effective as surgical treatment while the dilemma of grade II
acromioclavicular injury continues.

Cox (1981) studied 164 acromioclavicular
joint injuries at the US Naval Academy: of
these, 99 were grade 1, 52 were grade II, and
13 were grade III. Follow-up examination revealed that 36 percent of grade I, 48 percent of
grade II and 69 percent of grade III patients
had residual symptoms. He suggested that
aggressive treatment and rehabilitation
should be indicated in acute acromioclavicular injuries and advocated the use of an
acromioclavicular immobilizer in the treatment of grade II injuries.

Cox (1991) reported on the current methods
of treatment of acromioclavicular joint injuries. He concluded that the current preferred
method of treatment of uncomplicated complete dislocation of the acromioclavicular
joint, grade III, is by the nonoperative method

wherein most surgeons preferred symptomatic treatment rather than reduction and immobilization for this injury as he had stated in 1981. The more complicated dislocation such as the grade IV and grade V required a surgical treatment of their choice. However, most recommended against primary excision of the distal clavicle.

Most, if not all, surgeons agree that if the clavicle tents the skin it should be reduced, repaired, and transfixed. There are many techniques for repairing this joint, but the author's preference is to reduce the clavicle in the acromion, remove the meniscus if disrupted, transfix the acromion to the clavicle with stout threaded pins, repair the capsule and the superior acromioclavicular ligament, and carry out a pants-over-vest imbrication of the trapezius and deltoid muscles. Isometric exercise should commence and is maintained until the pins are removed after 6 weeks. Motion is then started, coupled with a rehabilitative program.

Closed reduction and external support have been suggested to manage a complete disruption of the acromioclavicular joint. The author does not, however, support this technique for a number of reasons:

- The straps utilized are difficult to maintain and the reduction may be and, usually is, lost.

- Pressure sores over the acromion and elbow are a common occurrence.

- If pain or disability remains after healing of the dislocation, thus inhibiting the patient's activities of daily living, a resection of the distal end of the clavicle with double breasting of the osteoperiosteal capsular and muscular flaps for stability is the method of choice of most surgeons.

Early in my career I thought that all complete dislocations, particularly of an athlete, had to be reduced openly and fixed in place. It became evident that a number of these individuals continued to have discomfort, thus necessitating a resection of the distal end of the clavicle. When this situation is coupled with the fact that serendipitously, there were patients who refused surgery and then had complete use of their extremity — including pitchers at a major league level — it became evident that a closed or open reduction of the clavicle is not indicated except in the instance where the skin is tented by the clavicle.

Osteolysis

Osteolysis of the distal end of the clavicle occurs and is a cause of shoulder pain. Rockwood and Green (1984) noted in a series of 100 cases that osteolysis did not occur in women and that the majority occurred in weightlifters. Other authors have reported an acute injury as the cause, with repeated stress as another causative factor. Most athletes with osteolysis do not have an acute injury; however, I have observed the condition in a professional baseball player who sustained a grade II injury when he crashed into a wall with the point of his shoulder. One year later, an X-ray, taken for a new injury to the opposite shoulder, revealed asymptomatic osteolysis of the previously injured shoulder. The author has treated two women with this condition following acute trauma.

Cahill (1982), in his discussion of osteolysis of the distal clavicle in male athletes, noted the onset of osteolysis without the history of acute injury to the area. All his patients were athletes and 45 lifted weights as part of their training. They had pain and tenderness about the acromioclavicular joint, with associated radiologic signs of osteoporosis, loss of subchondral bone detail, and cystic changes in the distal part of the clavicle. Bone scans revealed increased activity in all patients. If the patient ceased weightlifting activity or changed their sports activity, including the avoidance of weight training, they had relief of their symptomatology. If they continued to exercise, then a resection of the distal end of the clavicle was necessary for relief of symptoms. All but 5 of 21 patients operated on by Cahill returned to their sports activity and weight training.

Brunet et al (1986) has reported a case of atraumatic osteolysis of the distal clavicle in a young male baseball pitcher who supplemented his sport with a weightlifting program; he suggests a synovial pathogenesis as the cause of atraumatic osteolysis. Levine suggested the possibility that a post-traumatic process arose from the synovium.

10
The glenohumeral joint

Functional anatomy

The glenohumeral joint belongs to the ball-and-socket group of synovial joints. There is no joint in the body with movements so free and varied as those in the shoulder joint.

Freedom of shoulder movement is provided in two ways: by the large size of the humerus in comparison with the small glenoid cavity, and by the laxity of its capsule. This freedom of movement can lead to the stability of the joint being contradicted; however, its stability does not lie with the adaption of the bony surfaces to one another nor in the strength of its ligaments. It lies in the powerful muscles that closely surround it; the coracocromial arch, which overhangs it to form a secondary superhumeral articulation preventing superior displacement; the articular glenoid labrum; the glenohumeral ligaments; and the capsule. These structures, plus the musculature about the shoulder, interact to provide stability to the glenohumeral joint. The containment mechanism, as advocated by Howell and Galinat (1987), is composed of the articular glenoid, labrum, and glenohumeral ligaments combining to create a fibrocartilaginous socket of finite depth. This composite focuses the obliquely applied muscle forces acting to precisely center the humeral head in the glenoid. When the glenoid mechanism is disrupted (labral tear, glenoid rim fracture, attenuating glenohumeral ligaments), then muscle forces can no longer center the head. Reconstruction of the containment mechanism should be the goal of surgical management of the unstable shoulder.

Shoulder capsule

The capsule is supported on all aspects, except inferiorly, by a group of muscles and tendons adherent to it: above, there is the supraspinatus; behind, the infraspinatus and teres minor; and the subscapularis in front. Inferiorly, the capsule is unsupported by muscles, and in the ordinary dependent position of the limb, it bulges downwards forming a fold in the upper part of the quadrangular space (*Figure 10.1*).

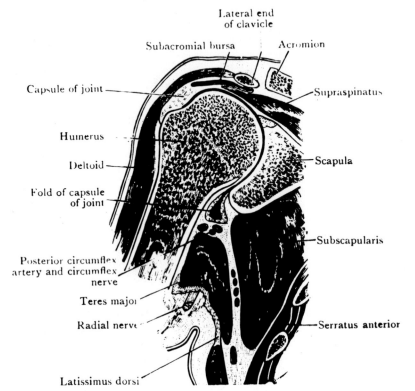

Lateral end
of clavicle

Subacromial bursa

Acromion

Capsule of joint

Supraspinatus

Humerus

Deltoid

Scapula

Fold of capsule
of joint

Posterior circumflex
artery and circumflex
nerve

Subscapularis

Teres major

Radial nerve

Serratus anterior

Latissimus dorsi

Figure 10.1

Coronal section through
shoulder, demonstrating
shoulder capsule (courtesy
of *Cunningham's Practical
Manual of Anatomy*, 1949,
p. 111).

Capsular ligaments

The capsular ligaments are thin, fairly dense
structures, enveloping the joint on all sides.
They are attached to the scapula about the
margin of the glenoid neck, fusing with the
outer surface of the glenoid labrum. Laterally,
the capsule is attached to the anatomical neck
of the humerus and to the transverse ligament
of the shoulder joint which bridges the top of
the bicipital groove to the intertubercular ligament. The other capsular ligament, the coracohumeral ligament, is a wide strong band on

the upper surface of the joint arising from the
outer border of the horizontal limb of the
coracoid process passing forward and downward in the interval between the supraspinatus and the subscapularis muscle. Its fibers
interlace with those of the fibrous capsule and
insert with the capsule into both tuberosities.
In this position, it acts as a suspensory ligament of the humeral head. The most proximal
fibers are arranged so that they unwind and
elongate on external rotation of the shaft of the
humerus, thereby functioning as a check rein
to external rotation.

Ferrari (1990), in an anatomical function study of the anterior–superior capsule of the shoulder, noted that the capsule had a distinct Z pattern with a prominent middle glenohumeral ligament evident in 88 percent of the shoulders, which probably combined DePalma's types I, II, III and possibly VI. **The Z-pattern included the coracohumeral ligament which has attachment to the superior glenohumeral ligament**.

Anatomists regard the superior glenohumeral ligament as the inferior portion of the coracohumeral ligament. Ferrari stated that the superior glenohumeral, coracohumeral, middle glenohumeral, and inferior glenohumeral ligaments formed an identifiable Z-pattern that functions through a range of abduction, external rotation, and extension. The middle glenohumeral and coracohumeral ligaments support the dependent arm. The coracohumeral ligament functions with the capsule and aids in the restraint of external rotation at 60° or less of abduction. The middle glenohumeral ligament was identifiable in most specimens but a small percentage of individuals have a weak or absent ligament. The large capsular opening occasionally seen in shoulder repairs is due to an absent or attenuated middle glenohumeral ligament. The clinical relevance of this is that in the shoulder, the proximal capsule functions in restraining external rotation. This is demonstrated by noting that a greater degree of external rotation could be obtained at 90° of abduction, less at 60°, and still less with the arm at the side. The anterior superior capsule could be stretched by placing the arm in extension and external rotation and gradually abducting, starting with the arm at the side through the range of abduction of less than 90°. A humeral head that dislocates or subluxates in this position is the result of weakened anterior superior capsular ligamentous structures.

The middle glenohumeral and anterior superior capsule can be stretched by heavy lifting that occurs in a position of external rotation, extension, and slight abduction, such as that utilized in the bench press. This may explain injuries from heavy weightlifting and bench pressing. The anterior attachment of the coracohumeral ligament that supports the biceps tendon becomes taut in extension and external rotation, correlating with the clinical findings that a fall backward with the arm extended may produce recurrent subluxation of the biceps tendon. **The break in the continuity of the cuff between the supraspinatus and the subscapularis tendon created by the coracohumeral ligament provides an excellent surgical approach to the inside of the glenohumeral joint.**

Glenohumeral ligaments

As previously noted, there are three glenohumeral ligaments: superior, middle, and inferior. These are thickened strands of capsule which reinforce the anterior portion of the capsule and act as static check reins to external rotation of the humeral head. This is important in throwing sports since these ligaments are stretched frequently causing excessive external rotation; therefore subluxation of the humeral head with resultant damage to the anterior glenoid labrum and rotator cuff tendons, particularly the supraspinatus.

The superior ligament blends with the superior portion of the labrum and biceps tendon, while the middle and inferior ligaments blend with the labrum at a lower level.

The middle glenoid ligament is a well-formed, distinct structure in most instances. When present, it arises from the anterior portion of the labrum immediately below the superior ligament.

The superior glenohumeral ligament is the most constant of the three ligaments. DePalma (1983) found it to be present in all but two of the specimens he examined. It arises from the upper pole of the glenoid fossa and the root of

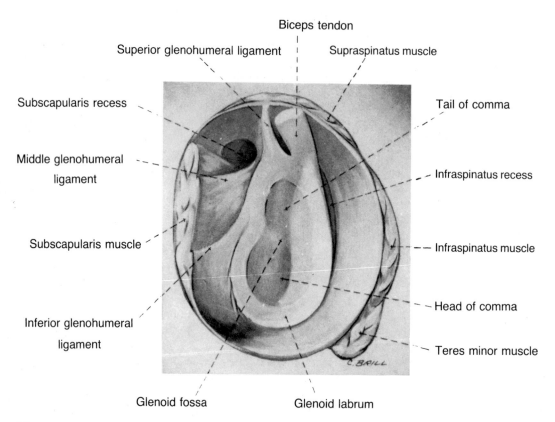

Figure 10.2

Glenoid labrum including superior glenohumeral
ligament and biceps tendon relationship (courtesy
of DePalma 1983, p. 57).

the coracoid process and is attached to the labrum and biceps tendon. This is important, since the superior ligament, together with the biceps tendon, exerts a distracting force on the labrum causing the labrum to pull away from the tail end of the glenoid (*Figure 10.2*).

The inferior glenohumeral ligament is a triangular structure with its apex at the labrum and its base blending with the capsule in the region between the subscapularis and the triceps tendon.

The glenoid fossa and the glenoid labrum

The glenoid fossa is shaped like an inverted comma. The superior portion designated the tail of the commo is narrow, while the inferior portion is broad. The fossa is covered by articular cartilage, which is thinner in the center than at the outer margins of the articular cavity.

The glenoid labrum, a fibrous structure, is triangular in cross section and rims the glenoid cavity. It is analogous to a knee meniscus. It deepens the glenoid cavity and adds support to the joint.

Acute injuries to the glenohumeral area

Dislocations

Dislocations of the shoulder are anterior and posterior, with anterior dislocations being the most common. Unfortunately, the rare posterior dislocation is commonly missed and therefore deserves significant attention since missing it predisposes to significant functional disability of the shoulder.

A study of over 2000 randomly selected citizens in Sweden ranging from ages 18 to 70 revealed the primary incidence of shoulder dislocation to be 1.7 percent. The lesion was three times more common in men between the ages of 21 and 31 than in men of other age groups. The male-to-female ratio with primary dislocation was 9:1.

It is generally accepted that the most important factor for recurrence of a primary dislocation is the age of the patient; however, there is wide disagreement about the incidence of recurrence. Rowe and Sakellarides (1961) reported a recurrence rate of 94 percent between the ages of 10–20; 79 percent for ages 21–30; 50 percent for ages 31–40; and 14 percent for ages 51–60. Kazar and Relovsky (1969) in their study revealed a recurrence rate for ages 10–20 of 50 percent; 21–30, 30 percent; 31–40, 7 percent; and 51–60, only 3 percent. Of the recurrent dislocations 70 percent occurred within two years.

Should a primary dislocation be immobilized and for how long? This is a controversial point in the treatment of primary dislocations. Many years ago it was given that the shoulder should be immobilized for approximately 6 weeks. Time, however, has shown that when one has the courage to discontinue immobilization following the cessation of pain, the incidence of re-dislocation in most studies is not any greater than with longer periods of immobilization. McLaughlin and MacLellan (1967) found no evidence to support the notion that immobilization changed the prognosis for recurrent dislocation. Allman (1978) is in favor of early mobilization. Prior to the prospective study of Hovelius (1978) the numbers of recurrent dislocation were retrospective studies. Hovelius, in a prospective study of primary dislocation occurring in patients age 40 and younger, separated the population into two groups. One group was immobilized for one week with a sling and the second group was treated by fixing the arm to the side of the body for 3–4 weeks. At the end of two years, the patients were examined again and it was noted that there was no statistical evidence that immobilization of a primary dislocation for 3–4 weeks when compared with the group in a sling for 1 week prevented chronic shoulder instability in any age group. It is my opinion that this is true, and for years I have treated people with immobilization in a sling until pain was relieved. Isometric exercises are performed during immobilization, followed by a program of graduated mobilization of the shoulder. To date, we have not seen any alarming difference in the rate of recurrence.

It should be noted that the bony configuration of the glenohumeral joint provides no stability. Stability of the joint depends upon the integrity of its capsule, its ligamentous structures, and the muscles about the joint, and also on a delicate neuromuscular balance, particularly of the rotator cuff musculature. The location of the joint and its participation in almost every movement of the shoulder girdle renders it vulnerable to many forms of trauma. Its proximity to the neurovascular structures can render these elements vulnerable to serious injury when the joint is injured. The glenohumeral ligaments play an important role in stability of the glenohumeral joint, particularly in recurrent dislocation and subluxation.

Two layers of muscles envelop the joint, an outer and inner layer which function in the manner of sleeves. The inner layer consists of the short rotators while the outer layer includes the deltoid, teres major, and pectoralis major. Abduction and flexion of the humerus are provided by the synchronous action of these two muscle groups. The shorter rotator group constitutes a functional unit that compresses the humeral head and fixes it firmly against the glenoid fossa, enabling the other group to flex and abduct the arm. The infraspinatus and teres minor play a small role in forward flexion; however are important in external rotation activity.

Mechanisms of injury

If rotation of the arm is obstructed during elevation of the arm, such as in abduction, forward flexion, and external rotation, the greater tuberosity abuts against the acromion and locks in this position. Forcing the arm beyond this locked position results in destruction of the soft tissue of the joint, a fracture of the humerus, or a combination of both.

Anterior dislocation occurs when a person falls on the outstretched arm or is trying to block a force such as a ball or another arm with the leverage applied to the arm in a fixed position of abduction and external rotation (*Figure 10.3*). A posterior dislocation occurs when the arm is below the horizontal and is flexed and internally rotated beyond the limits of the locked position (*Figure 10.4*).

How extensively the capsular ligaments and musculotendinous cuff are stretched depends upon the intensity of the forces acting on the various mechanisms. There are certain inherent mechanisms that tend to protect the glenohumeral joint from such disruptive forces. The prompt response of different muscle groups working synchronously positions the glenoid fossa squarely against the head of the humerus. This, in association with the ability of the scapula to glide and recoil freely on the thorax upon impact of a disruptive force, is an important factor: if the protective mechanism of the musculature is caught off guard or if the force applied is great enough to overcome it, then varying grades of sprains occur. These sprains are caused by forces transmitted to the shoulder driving it into an abducted, externally rotated position.

Grade I

A grade I sprain is defined as stretching of the ligaments with some tearing of the fibers; however, the continuity of structures remain

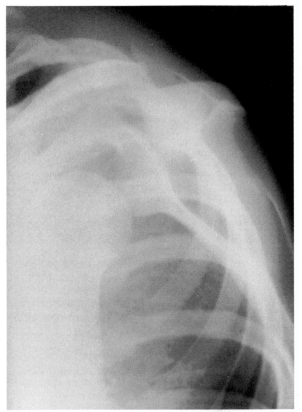

Figure 10.3

Radiographic view demonstrating anterior dislocation.

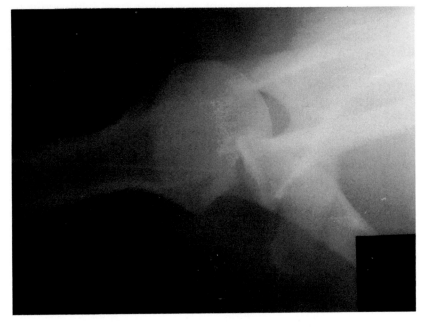

Figure 10.4

Radiographic view demonstrating posterior dislocation.

intact. **This injury is not entirely benign as it can go on to cause recurrent anterior subluxation.**

Grade II sprain and subluxation

By definition, a grade II injury is produced by a greater force acting than produced the grade I sprain. The head is levered over the rim of the glenoid fossa as it stretches and tears the capsular ligaments; however, it does not force the humeral head out of the glenoid cavity. It is readily reversed and the head slips back into the cavity. Stretching and tearing of the ligaments are sufficient to permit recurrent subluxation of the humeral head. The tears may occur anywhere in the capsule or at the attachment of the capsule along the glenoid rim; they are, however, incomplete so that the greater portion of the capsule remains intact. This is a severe injury and is the most common cause of recurrent subluxation and dislocation in young adults.

Grade III sprain and dislocation

A grade III injury is produced by the same mechanism as any grade II sprain but with greater force. The force is initiated at the humeral head, arm, or elbow and it drives the arm into extreme abduction and external rotation. The humeral head is forced against the anterior capsule or muscular buttress beneath the coracoacromial ligament. The neck of the humerus impinges upon the acromion and as the force continues, the muscular strength of the anterior buttress is overcome and the humeral head is levered out of the glenoid fossa. This is the most common lesion in young adults.

Pathologic basis for recurrent dislocations

Various pathologic lesions are encountered and are categorized into three areas: capsular lesions, muscular lesions, and bony lesions.

Capsular lesions

Capsular lesions include:

- Rupture of the capsule at the glenoid or fracture of the rim of the glenoid — Bankart lesion

- Rupture of the capsule from the humeral neck

- Excessive laxity of the capsule secondary to a grade II sprain or repeated injury

The majority of investigators agree that the most common lesion encountered, accounting for recurrent dislocation and subluxation of the shoulder, is a loss of stability along the rim of the glenoid due to avulsion of the capsule and labrum from the rim; this is the Bankart lesion. While not the essential lesion, it is the most common causative lesion of recurrent dislocation.

An abnormal redundancy of the inferior capsule is present in all individuals with subluxation of the humerus. The degree of the redundancy is determined at surgery with the shoulder in complete external rotation. If the capsule can be elevated 0.5 cm, it is considered mildly lax. If it can be lifted 1 cm, it is moderately lax. Anything beyond 1 cm is severely lax. Rowe (1988), DePalma (1983), and others consider the capsular laxity one of the essential lesions or causative factors in shoulder instability.

Muscular lesions

Some investigators have proposed that the subscapularis muscle is the primary cause of shoulder instability. It should be noted that in almost every sugical procedure for recurrent dislocation, it has a normal appearance.

The investigative contributions of Turkel et al (1981) concluded that in the lower range of abduction, the subscapularis muscle, the superior capsular ligament, and the coraco-humeral ligament stabilized the joint to a large extent. From 0–45° abduction, the joint is protected by the subscapularis, the middle glenohumeral ligament, and the superior fibers of the inferior capsular ligament. At 90° of abduction, the inferior capsular ligaments are the main restraint to anterior instability of the joint.

Bone lesions

A Hill–Sachs lesion is an impacted or compression fracture of the head of the humerus. Palmer and Widen (1948) concluded the Hill–Sachs lesion of the humeral head to be the essential lesion of recurrent anterior dislocation (*Figure 10.5*). This is to be considered as one of the causative lesions of recurrent dislocation rather than the essential lesion. Rowe et al (1978), in a follow-up study, found a Hill–Sachs lesion of the humeral head in 77 percent of 142 traumatic dislocations, in 40 percent of traumatic subluxators, and in 76 percent of failed surgical repairs. It was absent in voluntary dislocation. A Hill–Sachs lesion is produced by the recoil impaction or compression of the humeral head against the rim of the glenoid at the time of dislocation.

Fractures of the glenoid rim occur, according to Rowe, in 73 percent of traumatic dislocation. This is another causative factor in recurrent dislocation of the shoulder.

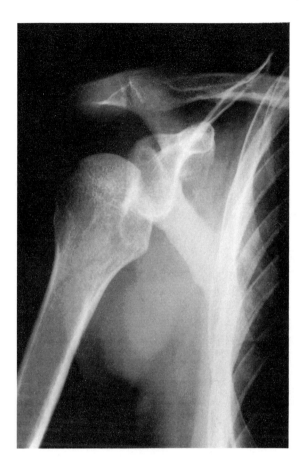

Figure 10.5

Radiographic view demonstrating Hill–Sachs lesion.

Table 10.1

Classification of dislocations.

Acute traumatic lesions
Anterior
Posterior
Multidirectional
   Traumatic
   Atraumatic

Unstable glenohumeral joint
Anterior recurrent dislocation
   Post-traumatic involuntary
   Atraumatic
   Voluntary
   Congenital
Posterior recurrent dislocation
   Post traumatic
   Atraumatic
   Voluntary
   Congenital

Recurrent subluxation
Traumatic subluxation
   Anterior, posterior
   Multidirectional instability
Atraumatic subluxation
   voluntary
      with psychologic problem
      without psychologic problem
   involuntary multidirectional
   congenital

Classification of dislocations

Dislocations can be classified into several groups (Table 10.1).

Treatment of shoulder dislocations

While closed reduction is easily accomplished with recurrent dislocation and, in fact, is most often carried out by the patient, in an initial dislocation it can be difficult to perform because of associated muscle spasm. There are many methods of reduction, but it would seem that a modification of the Kocher method referred to as the external rotation method is the one which usually will effect a reduction without undue complications. This should be performed very gently and should be preceded by the use of an injectable relaxant amnesic agent. The elbow is fixed to 90° and the arm is slowly adducted to the patient's side. Once this is achieved, it is slowly externally rotated, stopping every few degrees, until the spasm and resistance is overcome. By the time external rotation is complete, reduction occurs. Another method of reduction is the Simpson method, which employs the same principles of relaxation of the muscles in flexion. As previously stated, immobilization in a sling until pain is relieved, coupled by isometric exercise with the arm at the side, is initiated. Once the pain is relieved, a program for regaining motion, muscular tone, and strength is to commence.

Recurrent dislocation and subluxation of the shoulder

It is important to mention there are three areas of concern with recurrent dislocation and subluxation: capsular lesions, muscular lesions, and bony lesions.

Once a dislocation or subluxation becomes recurrent and is functionally disabling; the treatment choices are: a rehabilitative program, which may vary in its effectiveness; or a surgical stabilization.

Once the dislocation recurs three or more times, a reconstructive procedure is necessary, particularly in individuals active in sports. After a third dislocation, I counsel the individual towards a surgical procedure, since further rehabilitation frequently proves unsuccessful in eliminating dislocation. It should be understood that only if functional disability occurs should an operative procedure be considered.

With recurrent subluxation, pain and instability may inhibit the functional capacity of an athlete. In this situation we suggest reconstructive surgery if a rehabilitative program fails.

Once the decision is made to perform surgery with recurrent dislocation or subluxation, a surgical procedure of proven efficacy must be utilized. The most common procedures employed are listed; however, the details are not discussed, since there are reference books dedicated to these procedures and these should be referred to. Procedures include:

- Repair of capsule and labrum back to the glenoid rim (Bankart procedure)

- The capsulolabral repair advocated by Jobe

- Arthroscopic procedures (Gaspari–Morgan–Warren)

- Muscle and capsule plication (Putti–Platt)

- Muscle and tendon sling procedures (Magnuson–Stack); procedure modifications (Bristow–Helfet–Latrajet)

- Bone block (Eden–Hybbinette procedure)

- Osteotomies (Weber) — Humeral neck (Saha) — (humeral shaft)

- Capsulorrhaphies (Neer — anterior–inferior and posterior capsular shifts; Rowe — glenoid capsulorrhaphy)

The most commonly used procedures are the Bankart procedure as advocated by Rowe (1988, pp. 190–216, 235–7), the capsulolabral repair as advocated by Jobe et al (1991), the Bristow procedure modifications, and the Neer anterior–inferior and posterior capsular shift. The procedures involving bone blocks, osteotomies, and muscle transplants to the humeral head are for special situations. The author's procedure of choice is an anterior capsular repair for recurrent dislocation. The Neer anterior–inferior capsular shift is used for anterior subluxation, and the posterior capsular shift for posterior subluxation.

Arthroscopic suture repairs for anterior instability as advocated by Gaspari, Morgan, and Warren are presently being performed by many orthopaedists.

Morgan's technique for recurrent, traumatic anterior instability, utilizing arthroscopic surgical techniques (Morgan and Boderstab 1987), is depicted in *Figures 10.6–10.10*.

His indications are recurrent traumatic anterior instability, with the contraindications being multidirectional, atraumatic, or voluntary instability. The relative contraindications given by Morgan are those athletes involved in contact sports since excellent results were found in 83 percent, with poor results in 17 percent of that group. This is an excessively high rate of poor results. High-performance athletes cannot tolerate this possibility of obtaining a poor result. The other relative containdications are generalized laxity and excessive external rotation on the opposite unaffected side.

In a 3–6 year follow-up study of 57 patients, 96 percent had excellent results. In the most recent study by Morgan (1989), he included recurrent traumatic anterior subluxation along with recurrent traumatic anterior dislocation. A 1–3 year follow-up study of 98 patients revealed 93 percent excellent results. With the inclusion of more patients and then looking at the 1–6 year follow-up study of 161 patients, 95 percent of those had excellent results.

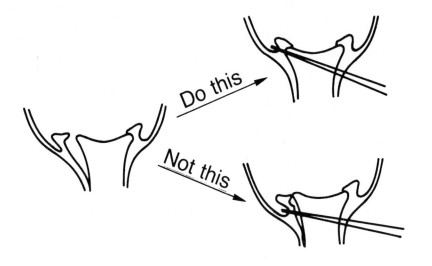

Figure 10.6

Arthroscopic surgical
technique for recurrent
traumatic anterior
instability (courtesy of
Craig Morgan, MD); see
further *Figures 10.7–10.10.*

Figure 10.7

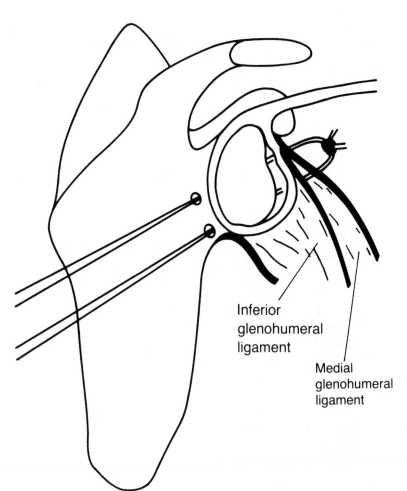

Inferior
glenohumeral
ligament

Medial
glenohumeral
ligament

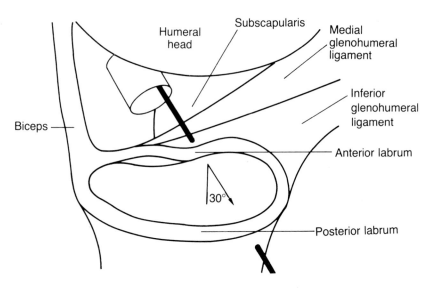

Figure 10.8

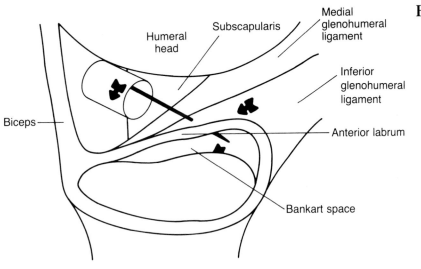

Figure 10.9

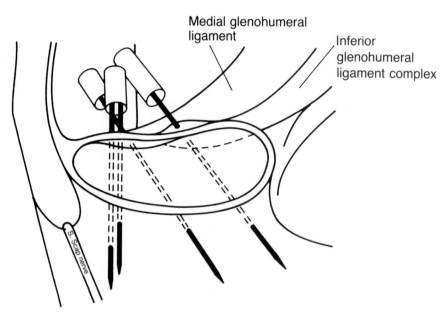

Figure 10.10

It should be noted that this arthroscopic procedure is an exacting technique with a high learning-curve. It should not be performed as an occasional procedure.

Glenoid lesions

Lesions of the superior labrum from anterior to posterior are known as SLAP (*Figure 10.11*). Arthroscopy is the only effective mode to diagnose and treat a SLAP lesion; however, MRI is a diagnostic modality.

Type I SLAP lesion

The superior labrum in a type I SLAP lesion has marked fraying with degenerative appearance but remains firmly attached to the glenoid. Treatment is debridement of the area.

Type II SLAP lesion

Type II lesions are very controversial and the most difficult to treat. The superior

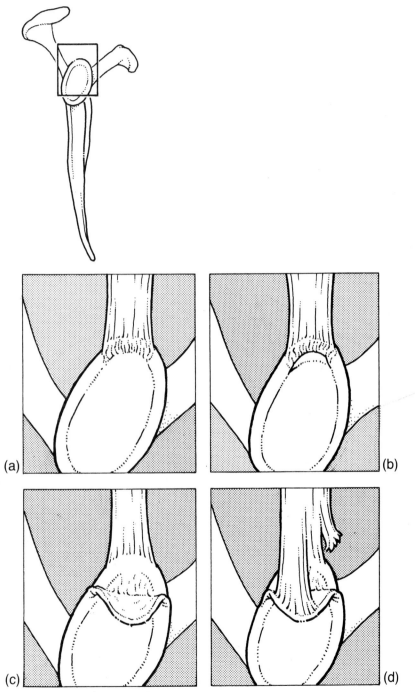

Figure 10.11

SLAP lesions: (a) type I, (b) type II, (c) type III,
(d) type IV.

labrum and biceps tendon are stripped off the underlying glenoid labrum. After the frayed labral tissue is debrided surgically, it is followed by abraiding beneath the biceps anchor to the supraglenoid portion so as to cause active bleeding for reattachment of the biceps tendon. The arm is then immobilized to allow the biceps labral complex to reattach.

Type III SLAP lesions

Type III SLAP lesions include bucket-handle tears of the superior labrum with an intact biceps anchor. The treatment is excision of the labral fragment.

Type IV SLAP lesion

In a type IV SLAP lesion a bucket-handle tear extends across the superior labrum into the biceps tendon. The labral and biceps fragments are usually excised.

Fractures of the glenohumeral area

Fractures of the scapula are rare injuries both in children and adults. In sports, they are very uncommon unless due to repeated stress. When they occur acutely, they are usually caused by violent injuries and are often difficult to detect on initial examination. Scapular fractures occur in approximately 5 percent of injuries about the shoulder. These occur in the body, through the glenoid neck, or through the coracoid process (*Figure 10.12*).

The fractures about the coracoid process are usually seen in violent injuries such as automobile accidents, in association with multiple other fractures including severe chest trauma.

The isolated injury to the coracoid process of the scapula usually occurs following a stress reaction. There have been a number of cases reported and recently a fracture of the base of the coracoid process occurred in a professional major league baseball pitcher while throwing a pitch in a game. The fact that this problem occurred acutely did not negate the fact that this player had complained of discomfort about the shoulder approximately three weeks prior to the development of the fracture. He also was involved in a rather vigorous conditioning program that involved the upper extremities with weights, martial-arts activities, and repeated push-ups. Coracoid stress fractures have also been reported in trapshooters and tennis players.

Fractures of the body of the scapula are usually comminuted with minimal displacement. Operative reduction is seldom necessary; the use of a sling until comfortable with early motion is all that usually is required.

Fractures of the neck of the scapula are generally vertical from the suprascapular notch to the axillary border of the scapula. A nondisplaced fracture is of little consequence. The more severe injuries that are displaced require an open reduction.

Fractures of the glenoid may occur due to compression forces of the humeral head on the glenoid from a direct blow to the shoulder. Most surgeons recommend non-operative treatment with early motion. Operative reduction should be considered if there are large fragments displaced more than 1 cm since this displacement can lead to glenohumeral joint instability.

Fractures of the acromion lateral to the coracoacromial ligament are due to a direct blow and are undisplaced. Symptomatic treatment is all that is necessary. A fracture of the acromion should never be confused for an unfused acromial apophysis. If in doubt, the opposite shoulder should be examined radiographically.

Fractures of the coracoid are rare, as previously mentioned, and are usually treated in

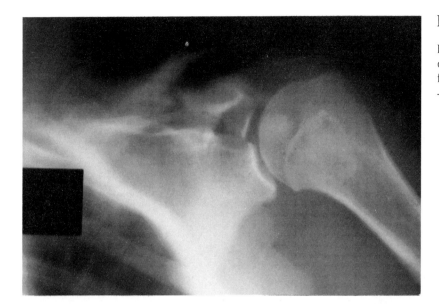

Figure 10.12

Radiographic view demonstrating glenoid fracture.

a nonoperative fashion. If a fracture is displaced and angulated to a significant degree, then an operative procedure may be indicated.

Proximal humeral fractures

Acute traumatic fractures of the humerus are uncommon injuries in the pediatric population; however, a stress fracture in an adolescent is fairly common. This injury is known as the little league shoulder and is a Salter-Harris I injury. Reduction is generally not necessary. In a Salter-Harris II injury with displacement, the rule of thumb would be to consider an attempt at reduction if angulation exceeds 35°. Results of treatment are generally good even if moderate amounts of angulation are accepted since the shoulder has the ability

to accept a small decrease in range of motion and the deltoid will cosmetically mask an angular deformity of the proximal humerus.

Little league shoulder is secondary to repeated stress and is likened to a slipped epiphysis of the femur. Fortunately, the results are not disastrous as in the hip and most cases are treated with a sling until there is enough callous to begin early motion. A stress reaction can occur in the proximal humerus below the epiphysis and has been seen not only in the adolescent with an open epiphysis but in adults, particularly in those who are into throwing sports such as baseball. A number of stress fractures of the proximal humerus occuring in young adult baseball pichers have been seen (*Figure 10.13*); these have been treated by closed methods with excellent results (*Figure 10.14*). Naturally, a rehabilitative program is necessary prior to returning to the sport.

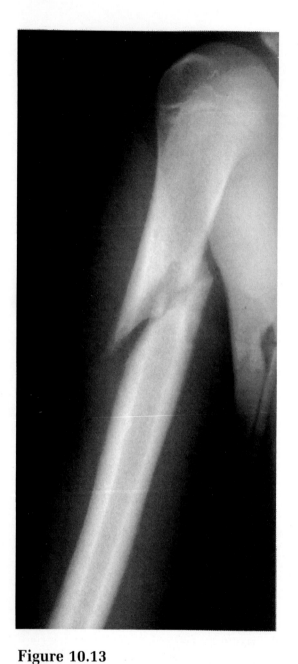

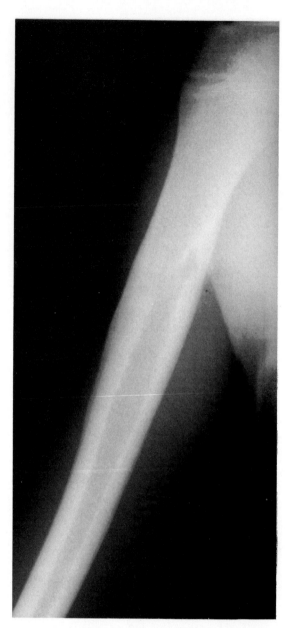

Figure 10.13

Fracture of proximal humerus in a young adult
baseball pitcher, demonstrated by a radiographic
view.

Figure 10.14

Fracture of proximal humerus in young adult
baseball pitcher treated with closed method prior
to commencement of rehabilitation program.

11
Rotator cuff disease

Functional anatomy

The rotator cuff musculature acts in unison to depress and stabilize the humeral head, while the supraspinatus acts in concert with the deltoid muscle in flexion of the shoulder in the scapular plane. The infraspinatus is a powerful external rotator while the subscapularis is a powerful internal rotator. The innervation of these muscles is as follows:

- Upper and middle subscapularis — the superior subscapular nerve
- Lower subscapularis — the inferior subscapular and axillary nerves
- Supraspinatus and infraspinatus — suprascapular nerve
- Teres minor — axillary nerve

Pathophysiology

The causation of rotator cuff disease is varied.

Supraspinatus impingement syndrome

Acromial anatomy

The anatomical configuration of the acromion has been implicated as a cause of impingement. There are three types namely, types I, II, and III, as noted in Table 11.1.

It should be noted that as the angle of inclination becomes more acute, it is associated with pathologic conditions of the rotator cuff. This angle is formed by a line joining the posterior–inferior aspects of the acromion and the anterior margin of the acromion with a line formed by joining the posterior–inferior aspect of the acromion and the inferior tip of the coracoid process. Various authors such as Morrison and Bigliani (1987) and Neer are proponents of the impingement causation of rotator cuff disease.

Risk factors for impingement and rotator cuff disease include: acromial contour/acromioclavicular prominance, greater tuberosity prominance, rotator cuff weakness, impaired singular suspension, and the coracoacromial ligament.

Table 11.1

Types of anatomical configuration of the acromion.

I — Relatively high angle or flat undersurface

II — Downard curve and a decreased angle of inclination

III — This has almost a hooked shaped configuration along the anterior portion of the acromion and a further reduction in the angle of inclination

---

Greater tuberosity prominence

A number of authors have noted that individuals with a prominent greater tuberosity have a decreased distance of the suprahumeral articulation, stating that it is another cause of rotator cuff disease secondary to impingement. Cystic–sclerotic changes have been seen on radiograph in many of these individuals (*Figure 11.1*).

Rotator cuff weakness

With rotator cuff weakness, there is a decrease in humeral compression forces which are

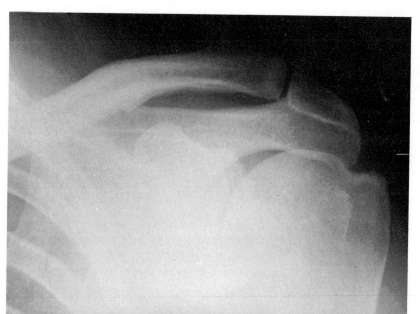

Figure 11.1

Cystic–sclerotic changes at greater tuberosity.

necessary to act in concert with the deltoid muscle in order to produce normal shoulder motion.

Coracoacromial ligament

The coracoacromial ligament has been implicated as a causation of rotator cuff disease. Some authors have advocated a division of the structure, while others advocate the excision of the ligament. This ligament seems to play an important part along with the shape of the acromion.

Vascular–degenerative causes

There is a hypovascular zone in the supraspinatus tendon, as advocated by Rathburn (1970), Rothman and Parke (1965), and others.

Tensile overload

Tensile overload or angiofibroplastic dysplasia is another theory, as advocated by Nirschl (1987).

Traumatic causation

There are number of causes of trauma involved in the etiology of rotator cuff disease. They are as follows:

- A displaced fracture of the greater tuberosity

- Anterior shoulder dislocation in the elderly

- Minor trauma superimposed on a degenerative tendon

- Massive sudden avulsion injury to the rotator cuff

- Repetitive overuse such as in the throwing athlete.

Diagnosis

While diagnosis of rotator cuff disease is made on a clinical basis, it must be supplemented by certain investigative techniques.

Physical examination reveals tenderness in the anterior aspect of the shoulder along with a decreased range of motion and a positive impingement syndrome. There is associated weakness of forward flexion implicating the supraspinatus muscle. If external rotation weakness is present, it implies that a large tear is also present since it involves the infraspinatus muscle. The diagnostic aids utilized in the diagnosis of rotator cuff disease include radiographs, arthrography, MRI, ultrasonography, and arthroscopy.

Radiographs

A sclerotic greater tuberosity may be seen on plain radiographs, along with an anatomical abnormality of the acromion which may be visualized with a lateral view or oblique view. There may be spurring at the acromial insertion of the coracoacromial ligament or arthritic changes in the acromioclavicular joint (*Figure 11.2*).

Shoulder arthrography

Shoulder arthrography was once considered to be the gold standard in the diagnosis of rotator cuff disease (*Figure 11.3*). More rec-

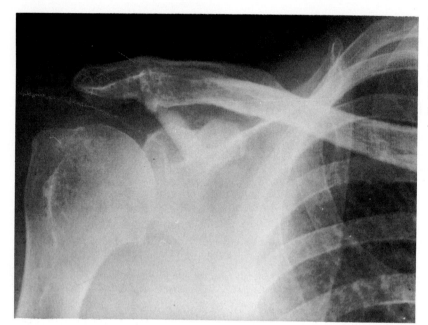

Figure 11.2

Spurring and sclerotic
change at acromion and
greater tuberosity,
demonstrated on
radiographic view.

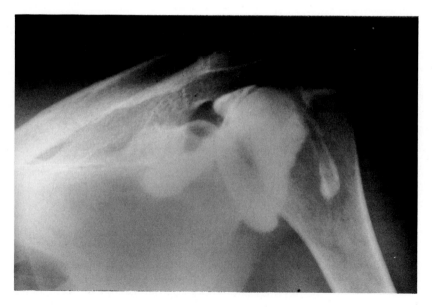

Figure 11.3

Shoulder arthrography.

ently, MRI has supplanted it in most institutions.

Magnetic Resonance Imaging

If MRI is performed at an institution with the proper machine and interpreted by an individual who is responsive to and responsible for the task, it is a more sensitive and specific test than arthrography (*Figure 11.4*). In a study performed at Thomas Jefferson University Hospital by Horwitz et al (1989), it was determined that the advantages of MRI from an index study are that it is equally accurate as arthrography in detecting rotator cuff tears (92 percent sensitivity, 100 percent specificity, 94 percent accuracy), and therefore is the non-invasive test of choice. It was further determined that the MRI provided additional information that the arthrogram did not including accurate size determination, location of the tears, and identification of impingement lesions without actual tears. With the anatomic grading system employed, MRI was significantly more accurate than the arthrogram in retrospective evaluation of 25 patients with surgical correlation. Magnetic resonance imaging accurately determined rotator cuff disease in 18 of 25 patients while the arthrogram was correct in only 11 of 25 patients.

It should be noted that MRI is the most powerful diagnostic tool for rotator cuff disease including small partial tears and the ability to evaluate the amount of cuff atrophy present. With this in mind, MRI may be useful as a prognostic tool since once significant supraspinatus atrophy develops the prognosis is poor for recovery in rotator cuff disease.

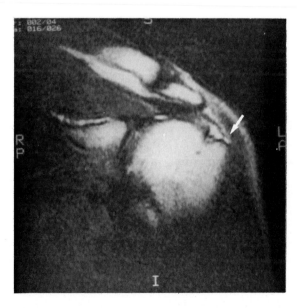

Figure 11.4

MRI scan, demonstrating complete or high-grade partial tear of left supraspinatus tendon proximal to its insertion on the greater tuberosity.

Ultrasonography

Ultrasonography is very technologist-dependent and less accurate than arthrography or MRI; however, it is non-invasive. It is less costly to perform and therefore more affordable but is not the author's choice as an investigative technique (*Figure 11.5*).

Arthroscopy

Arthroscopy is a valuable adjunct since it determines whether there is pathology within the joint. It not only indicates what is going on with small partial tears of the rotator cuff but

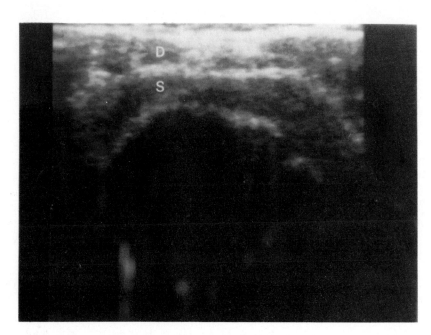

Figure 11.5

Ultrasonography of the shoulder: D, deltoid muscle; S, supraspinatus muscle.

also what, if anything, is affecting the labrum, the ligamentous structures, and the articular surface of the joint. The rotator cuff can be viewed from within and without or below and above (*Figure 11.6*).

MRI and throwing sports

It has been found that the MRI is useful with individuals involved in throwing sports. It will indicate not only rotator cuff disease but also other lesions.

In a recent study of MRI obtained for injuries sustained by professional baseball players by Burk et al (1989), it was noted that, because of the complex motion in throwing a baseball, a variety of stresses on the shoulder may lead to injury. These subtle injuries that may ensue may be apparent on MRI.

A starting professional baseball pitcher throws up to 200 pitches a game, performing 30–40 games within a season. The combination of contraction, relaxation, and stretching is apparent in the musculotendinous units, with the localization of forces at the tendon attachment. The cocking and acceleration phases of throwing place significant stress on the anterior aspect of the rotator cuff and may result in subluxation and impingement of the supraspinatus tendon with eventual cuff tear. The musculotendinous junction of the infraspinatus and teres minor is frequently inflamed secondary to the deceleration

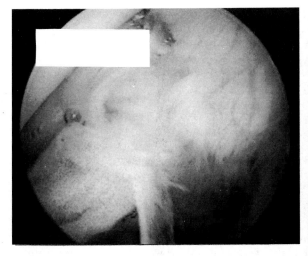

Figure 11.6

Arthroscopic surgery.

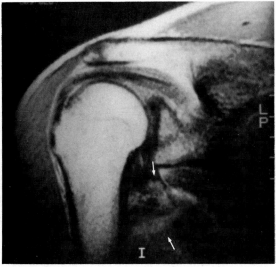

Figure 11.7

MRI scan depicting edema and swelling (arrows) of latissimus and teres major muscles at humeral insertion.

stresses of the follow-through motion. It produces tension forces on the posterior capsule and triceps tendon, causing a Bennett's lesion.

Magnetic resonance imaging has the ability to evaluate the rotator cuff not only for tears of the cuff but also for atrophy of the musculature about the rotator cuff and other musculotendinous units involved in the throwing act. It can detect a fluid-filled gap in the rotator cuff tendons, bursal side tears, and tears at the distal insertion more effectively than arthrography. Even though the tears of the rotator cuff of the baseball players in this study were relatively small, the degree of disability in a high-performance athlete was significant and usually represented a career-threatening injury. Cortical irregularity and subchondral cystic changes in the posterior aspect of the

greater tuberosity were present in a large proportion of the players with and without rotator cuff tears. This was also noted in an asymptomatic pitcher who was included in the study.

There are other causes of shoulder pain in the throwing athlete which are difficult to evaluate with other techniques but can be diagnosed with MRI. Loose bodies, which are seen on plain radiography, can be accurately located within a specific area of the shoulder. Pure osteochondral fragments containing fatty marrow demonstrate a high signal intensity on T1-weighted imaging while sclerotic lesions have a low signal intensity on all pulsing sequences. Cartilagenous loose bodies, which often are invisible on T1-weighted images, can be detected on T2-weighted imaging. This, obviously, cannot be evaluated by plain radiography or arthography.

Muscle tears suspected from a clinical examination are difficult to confirm with most imaging studies. However, one baseball player in the study presented with an unusual complaint of pain in the shoulder when throwing a breaking ball; MRI revealed a strain of the teres major and latissimus dorsi muscle at their insertion into the humerus (*Figure 11.7*). Biceps tendon lesions and labral tears are evaluated very nicely with MRI techniques. Magnetic resonance imaging demonstrated high levels of sensitivity, specificity, positive and negative predicted values and accuracy for evaluation of the glenoid labrum. **Magnetic resonance imaging is a reliable and accurate method for depicting the status of the glenoid labrum**.

The examination of labral and muscle/tendon structures is dependent upon high-quality axial images, which are easy to obtain with recent improvements in surface coil technology. There is no doubt that MRI is a valuable intermediate diagnostic step between plain radiography and arthroscopy in the evaluation of shoulder pain. The non-invasiveness of MRI lends itself to the performance of longitudinal studies of professional athletes in the future, which will be of benefit in determining the natural history of these career-threatening shoulder injuries.

Impingement syndrome in throwing athletes

Rotator cuff tears can be divided into two separate diseases. 'One for the older population (over 35 years of age) and another for the younger population (18–35 years). The older age group has a high degree of pure impinge-

ment with associated rotator cuff tear. In the young athlete, however, the most common cause of shoulder dysfunction is anterior instability due to inherent increased range of motion demands of the overhead sport, leading to secondary impingement. Very few patients in the young age group have a pure impingement, and careful examination delineates this.

When the ligamentous and muscular structures are subjected to increased external rotation, velocity, force, and repetitive motion that is inherent in overhead sports, they are subjected to stress with consequent instability. The balance that integrates functional mobility and stability is sometimes disrupted. A chain reaction of asynchronous firing in the rotator cuff and scapular rotator muscles then ensues. This combination produces silent subluxation with secondary impingement. It is important to realize that impingement and instability are not two separate entities but a continuum of shoulder pathologies.

History and physical examination

The principal complaint reported in throwing athletes is anterior or posterior shoulder pain. The hallmark of a rotator cuff tear is night and rest symptoms, whereas in rotator cuff tendinitis it is pain with progressive shoulder activity. Pain that occurs simultaneously with a specific phase of throwing, particularly acceleration, should alert the examiner to look for instability mimicking or creating rotator cuff tendinitis. It would be remiss not to investigate the other causes of shoulder pain, such as cervical radiculitis, brachial plexus stretch, neurapraxia, thoracic outlet syndrome, or entrapment of the suprascapular nerve, axillary nerve, or musculocutaneous nerve. It is important to realize that these causes of shoulder pain also cause muscular weakness and imbalance.

Specific signs of impingement include pain over the anterior acromion and/or the greater tuberosity with a painful arc of abduction maximized at 90°. Neer forcibly forward-flexes the shoulder and simultaneously internally rotates it, causing the greater tuberosity to abut against the acromion. Hawkins et al (1988) position the arm at 90° of forward flexion and forcibly internally rotate the shoulder, impaling the supraspinatus tendon against the acromion. If xylocaine is injected beneath the acromion and the test is repeated, the pain is obliterated, although this will occur not only from pure impingement but with subluxation and impingement. While a number of orthopedists use this test we at the Thomas Jefferson Sports Medicine Center do not use it except under extraordinary circumstances.

Specific shoulder instability testing must be performed for every patient. As in the Lachman test for anterior cruciate deficiency of the knee, the examiner must have extensive experience to uncover silent subluxation. One test for anterior shoulder instability, the relocation test, is performed with the patient supine and the arm at 90° of abduction and external rotation with the arm free of the examining table. The examiner then pushes anteriorly on the posterior aspect of the humeral head while externally rotating the arm. If anterior subluxation is pathologic, it will cause pain. The test is then repeated with the humeral head held in place while the arm is externally rotated and abducted. If the pain that was present without holding the humeral head in place is relieved, this is excellent evidence of anterior subluxation as a cause of pain in the throwing act.

If the external abduction motion with the humeral head being pushed anteriorly causes apprehension rather than pain, traumatic subluxation or dislocation is strongly suggested. Jobe et al (1990) classified anterior shoulder pain into four groups:

- *Group I* — pure and isolated impingement

- *Group II* — impingement findings and concurrent instability due to chronic labral and capsular microtrauma (the most common cause of shoulder pain in the throwing athlete)

- *Group III* — those patients who have impingement findings and instability due to hyperelasticity in a lax joint

- *Group IV* — isolated instability due to blunt trauma without impingement; this is also known as 'traumatic anterior subluxation'

When the impingement syndrome occurs in throwing athletes, treatment consists of an intensive and specific exercise program, which has been found to be successful in the majority of cases: Jobe 1990 quotes a 95 percent success rate. It is wise to mention that specific exercises are excellent for injury prevention and therefore should be prescribed for all individuals involved with overhead sports.

The goal of a rehabilitation process is to restore the strength of the scapular rotators, rotator cuff, and positioning muscles, while permitting maximal range of motion. Once the muscles are strong, they are retrained to fire in a synchronous fashion for their specific sport activity. Initially, rest is instituted which consists of avoiding the overhead activity while not putting the arm in a sling. Anti-inflammatory agents are useful and at the Thomas Jefferson Sports Medicine Center we routinely use prednisone over a 6-day period commencing with 32 mg and finishing with 4 mg. Occasionally, an injection of a cortisone/xylocaine mixture is given for individuals with extremely painful shoulders; this injection must be in the subacromial space, not in the tendon or bursal tissue.

The internal and external rotator musculature is strengthened with the arm at the side isometrically, isotonically, and isokinetically. The forward flexors are strengthened, with limitation of forward flexion to just below the 90° plane. The pectoralis major and anterior deltoid are strengthened using horizontal adduction exercise which begin with the arm abducted to 90°. All exercise should be performed in the scapular plane with less than 90° of abduction. Humeral hyperextension is avoided because it places the head of the humerus in a vulnerable anterior position. Generally, stretching exercises are contraindicated with anterior instability. The posterior deltoid, posterior capsule, and rhomboids are tight, thus gentle mobilization of these structures is recommended.

If the rehabilitation process fails to act favorably after three months of a supervised program, an acromioplasty with resection of the coracoacromial ligament and thickened bursa is indicated in a pure impingement syndrome. This should be performed after arthroscopy confirms that there is no anterior subluxation of the humerus or a tear of the glenoid labrum. If anterior subluxation is an integral part of the impingement, an anterior capsular reconstruction is indicated. Arthroscopic findings may include: fraying of the rotator cuff; a torn or absent inferior glenohumeral ligament; a torn anterior and/or posterior labrum; a posterior humeral head defect; or an anterior inferior subluxation of the humeral head.

Complete rotator cuff tears with associated subluxation necessitate anatomic repair of the capsule with repair of the rotator cuff.

In Group II patients with impingement and instability secondary to chronic labral and capsular microtrauma or in Group III patients — those with impingement and instability due to hyperelasticity of the joint — surgery is recommended if a rehabilitative program does not work.

Classifications of tears

Many classifications of tears of the rotator cuff have been advanced. A tear can be incomplete, partial, or complete. Complete tears may be transverse, vertical, longitudinal, complex or massive with retraction. The size of a tear varies from a very small partial or complete tear to a large complete tear. A tear is considered small if it is between 1 and 3 cm, moderate between 3 and 5 cm, and large with anything greater than 5 cm.

The management of rotator cuff tears

The treatment of rotator cuff disease is either on an operative or nonoperative basis. The nonathlete usually responds more favorably to the nonoperative program than the young throwing athlete. Hawkins et al (1988) reported an 86 percent satisfactory result with the nonoperative treatment in 53 full thickness tears, however 94 percent of those had weakness in forward flexion and/or external rotation.

Although the operative treatment of rotator cuff disease has not changed much over the years, a new dimension has been added, namely, arthroscopic surgery. It should be noted that large, full-thickness rotator cuff tears are repaired by the open method.

Cofield (1987) stated that with the acute onset of pain, no matter how minor the trauma, there are three groups of individuals with regard to the timing of surgical care: the athlete or active individual who necessitates early diagnosis with early surgery; those individuals who are moderately active should be provided with conservative therapy for 3–6 weeks; and those who are inactive and should be given a more extensive conservative program prior to surgery. In this last group surgery is reserved for pain relief.

Whenever rotator cuff debridement and/or repair are performed, these should be accomplished with an acromioplasty. Ellman (1987) accentuates this statement since he noted 25 per cent of those who had debrided partial tears without an acromioplasty went on to a complete tear in the early postoperative period.

Arthroscopy followed by open repair for partial tears with instability has been advocated by some, particularly in the athlete with overhead activities. Some surgeons are of the opinion that arthroscopic debridement of the tear associated with an arthroscopic acromioplasty is all that is necessary. Andrews (et al 1984) stated that 85 percent of his athletes returned to their previous competitive level. This is questioned not only by this author but by others who have extensive experience in the treatment of athletes, particularly at a professional level. Ogilvie-Harris (1987) gives a more reflective outcome of this problem: he stated that 50 percent satisfactory results occur with arthroscopic treatment. Altchek (et al 1990) reported 66 percent good to excellent results following acromioplasty alone, whereas Gartsman (1988) reports an 83 percent satisfactory result.

Principles of repair with complete rotator cuff tears

The principles of repair with complete rotator cuff tears include:

- Adequate subacromial decompression

- Avoidance of shortening of the acromial process

- Adequate tension in repair (the arm should be at the side with the repair)

- Detachment of the deltoid?

On this last point, advocates of the deltoid detachment state that reattachment of the deltoid to the bone does not cause significant early or late problems. Those who advocate minimum to no deltoid detachment feel that it avoids postoperative weakness of anterior deltoid shoulder function.

Treatment of massive tears

Treatment of massive tears is a very controversial subject. It has, however, been noted by other authors and myself that a decompression is indicated for pain relief even if a repair can not be effected.

Bigliani reported 85 percent good-to-excellent results with repair of massive tears. He also noted that forward flexion improved from 88° to 164° on average.

Rockwood has extensive experience with cuff debridement. With acromioplasty he concludes (1987) that pain is relieved and there is an increase in forward flexion.

In conclusion, every reasonable effort should be made to repair rotator cuff disease, even if massive. Grafting of a large defect or transposition of the subscapularis is not worth the effort since pain relief can be obtained with debridement alone. Active range of motion, particularly forward flexion, may be limited following surgery for relief of pain and rotator cuff disease because of the weakness and dysfunction of the rotator cuff and the anterior deltoid muscle, and with the absence of the long head of the biceps muscle.

Results of arthroscopic shoulder decompression

Paulos and Franklin (1990) evaluated 80 consecutive subacromial decompressions in patients with impingement syndromes. The greatest improvements were seen in the area of pain relief with activity and in pain at night with a decrease in the use of medications. Repeat surgery was necessary in eight cases because of full thickness tears of the rotator cuff, laxity of the shoulder, and/or acromioclavicular problems. They found a number a unsuspected diagnoses during arthroscopy of the shoulder prior to the subacromial decompression. Twelve patients had significant labral tears, seven patients had complete rotator cuff tears, four patients had biceps tendon fraying, and two patients had loose bodies in the glenohumeral joint. Most, if not all, of these problems should not go undiagnosed today if MRI is utilized.

Altchek et al (1990) reported on 44 patients treated by arthroscopic acromioplasty. The average age was 43.2 years: 86 percent of those who participated regularly in sports had been disabled due to symptoms of impingement. All of the patients had a minimum of 6 months of nonoperative therapy. Of the group, 24 patients had stage II impingement, 6 had a partial thickness tear of the rotator cuff, and 10 had a full thickness tear of the rotator cuff. Postoperatively, good-to-excellent results occurred in 73 percent of the patients and the average return to their sporting activity was 2.4 months. It should, however, be noted that most of the patients were not athletes at a highly competitive level of throwing sports. The average time to full recovery was 3.8 months with no complications. Of the patients, 92 percent were satisfied with the result.

Failed acromioplasty with impingement syndrome

Ogilvie-Harris (1990) reported on 65 patients who had pain and discomfort for more than 2 years after an initial acromioplasty for impingement syndrome without a rotator cuff tear. Of the shoulders investigated, 27 were diagnostic errors and 28 operative errors, while the diagnosis and operative procedure were correct in 12. Subsequent operative intervention in patients not receiving worker's compensation benefits had a 75 percent success rate, whereas for those receiving benefits, the success rate was only 46 percent. Of the diagnostic errors, 25 percent were due to instability of the shoulder.

Comparative results of arthroscopic acromioplasty in rotator cuff disease vs open acromioplasty with repair

Arthroscopic acromioplasty associated with full-thickness tears does not give satisfactory short- or long-term results. Ellman (1987) reported 35 percent, Gartsman (1988) 50 percent, and Altchek et al (1990) 40 percent unsatisfactory results. With partial-thickness tears, the numbers of good results increased: Gartsman stated there were 17 percent unsatisfactory results, whereas Altchek reports 30 percent.

Esch, in his study of 102 patients (1989), who received arthroscopic acromioplasty, with a 1–3 year follow-up, indicated a satisfaction rate of 84 percent of 67 patients with stage II disease, and 91 percent of 35 patients with stage III disease. For both stage II and selected stage III disease, 80 percent of the results were rated excellent or good on the objective UCLA rating scale. His surgical indications were patients with Neer Stage II disease of the rotator cuff with failed conservative treatment. A type III acromion is usually present on the outlet view. Stage III disease, manifesting a complete but small tear of the rotator cuff in patients 45–60 years of age with no evidence of weakness, benefits from this procedure.

Acromioplasty with open repair of full-thickness tears in a large series with a long follow-up, had 84–91 percent excellent-to-good results. Fukada (1987) reported 92 percent satisfactory results with partial thickness tears.

Factors leading to poor results in rotator cuff surgery

The factors that lead to poor results in rotator cuff surgery are multiple and include:

- Multiple preoperative steroid injections
- Preoperative weakness in both forward flexion and external rotation
- Large cuff defects with or without a biceps tendon rupture
- Chronic symptomatology over 6 months
- Anterior deltoid weakness
- Misdiagnosed acromioclavicular joint or cervical spondylitic problems
- Splinting in abduction postoperatively
- Cuff arthropathy as evidenced by decreased acromiohumeral distance on a preoperative radiograph.

12
Neurologic problems

Neurologic involvement of the shoulder girdle

The free range of motion of the shoulder girdle with resultant traction, distraction, and compressive forces subjects the nerves about the shoulder girdle, from brachial plexus to peripheral nerves, to injury and entrapment syndromes. While these problems seem to occur as often in the amateur and professional athlete, they are more frequent in the amateur. The pain is described as radiating and burning in and about the shoulder girdle, with subjective or objective numbness. This is followed by functional instability of the upper extremity due to associated muscle weakness. Although pure shoulder pathology is not associated with pain extending below the insertion of the deltoid on the humerus, spinal cord injuries and cervical spine fractures do occur with spearheading football tackles or in falls wherein the head and shoulder are forced apart causing pain distal to the shoulder.

Acute brachial plexus involvement

Most cases of brachial plexus injuries are without motor loss and demonstrate paresthesias which resolve in a time span of minutes to several weeks. In some cases, paresthesias persist for months or even years after injury or inflammation. Early in the course of a brachial plexus injury, a transient slowing in conduction across the plexus or a mild prolongation of nerve latency, which improve as paresthesias begin to regress, may be seen.

There seems to be a relationship between brachial plexus injury and peripheral entrapment neuropathy.

Dyro (1983), after examining 1200 patients over a four-year period, found that 50 patients were diagnosed as having a brachial plexus lesion by history and electrophysiologic criteria. Traumatic lesions were present in 35, while a Parsonage–Turner syndrome was diagnosed in 15. Of those patients examined,

27 percent had complaints of paresthesias due to peripheral nerve entrapment and 24 percent had lesions requiring surgical correction. At the time of diagnosis of peripheral entrapment, these patients no longer had slowing of nerve conduction across the brachial plexus; therefore, this did not play a role in the continued complaints. Dyro's conclusion was that, following brachial plexus trauma, the peripheral nerve entrapments on the involved side were disruptions of axonal function proximal and distal as in the double-crush phenomenon.

Upton and McComas (1973), reporting on the double-crush syndrome, demonstrated a large number of patients with both carpal tunnel syndrome and cervical spine lesions which were diagnosed on a clinical and electrophysiologic basis. In essence, there is a net impairment of neural function because single axons injured in one region becomes more susceptible to damage at another site.

The Burner

The most common cervical spine injuries are those involving nerve roots and brachial plexus. The key to diagnosis of the burner injury is the short duration and the presence of pain with free range of motion of the cervical spine. Fortunately, most of these injuries are short-lived; however, occasionally axonotmesis occurs. If an individual complaining of a burning, tingling pain has resolution of this paresthesia and then demonstrates normal muscle strength of the upper extremity, he may return to the field, provided he has a pain-free range of motion of the cervical spine and upper extremity.

Speer and Bassett (1990) described six players in a single football season with burners that displayed a prolonged neurologic recovery. There was evidence of muscular weakness at 72 hours post injury that was best correlated with positive electrodiagnostic findings. Isokinetic strength evaluation demonstrated many relative strength differences that were difficult to discern with manual muscle testing. They concluded that the return of a player to athletic competition should be based on the clinical examination of the patient.

Acute cervical radiculopathy in weightlifters

Jordan et al (1990) reported acute cervical radiculopathy in three athletes with neck and shoulder girdle pain which radiated down the arm, associated with segmental weakness and paresthesia. Magnetic resonance imaging and cervical spine radiography revealed degenerative changes of the cervical spine. Once the symptoms subside with conservative management, the athlete was gradually allowed to resume activities, providing that there was no structural lesion of the cervical spine that would predispose to further injury. Typically, the C4–C7 area is involved with gradual degeneration which usually manifests itself insidiously during the fifth decade of life.

The abrupt onset of cervical radiculopathy in young patients in their series can be attributed to weightlifting trauma superimposed upon degenerative changes of the cervical spine.

The biomechanics responsible for the pathophysiology of acute cervical radiculopathy during weightlifting involve combined forceful hyperextension with axial loading of the cervical spine. The hyperextension probably increases neural/foramenal encroachment by osteophytic spurs. Axial loading produces compressive forces on the disc, thus precipitating herniation. Athletes with persistent cervical radiculopathy should not be involved with athletic participation until they have been thoroughly evaluated neurologically and with imaging techniques, in particular with MRI.

Cervical cord neurapraxia with transient quadriplegia

In cervical cord neurapraxia with transient quadriplegia, sensory changes occur that consist of burning pain and loss of sensation, associated with motor changes consistent with weakness or complete paralysis. This paralysis is transient in nature and complete recovery usually occurs within 10–15 minutes. At times, gradual resolution will occur over a two-day period. Neck pain is not present at the time of injury. The injury occurs with contact sports and early management is that of any cervical spine injury. Radiography will generally reveal pathology such as spinal stenosis, congenital fusion, cervical instability (*Figures 12.1, 12.2*) and chronic intervertebral disc disease.

Torg (1990), in a survey of 503 athletes participating in the NCAA Football Program, demonstrated an incidence of 1.3 cases of spinal stenosis per 10 000 individuals with 5 subjects of 39 373 reporting quadriplegia. It should be noted that athletes with diminution of the AP spinal diameter can, on forced hyperextension or hyperflexion, compress the spinal cord with transitory motor and sensory manifestations. There is no evidence that the occurrence of this injury predisposes the individual to permanent neurologic injury; however, individuals with this syndrome associated with cervical spine instability should be precluded from further participation in contact sports. Those with obvious spinal stenosis associated with congenital anomalies should be treated on an individual basis.

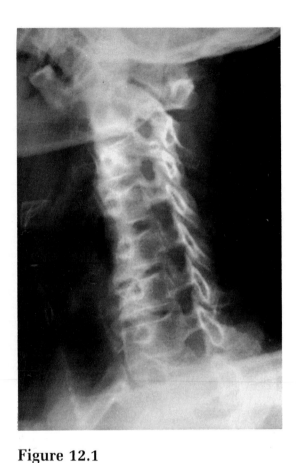

Figure 12.1

Radiographic anteroposterior view demonstrating cervical arthritis.

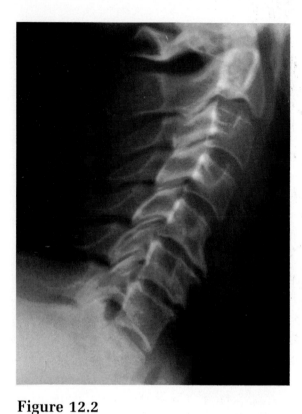

Figure 12.2

Radiographic lateral view demonstrating cervical arthritis.

Peripheral nerve involvement

Peripheral nerves are involved in acute injury and/or entrapment phenomena. The nerves involved, whether sensory, motor, or mixed, can cause different symptomatology and warrant further discussion.

The long thoracic nerve

The long nerve of Bell (long thoracic nerve) has been implicated in serratus anterior palsy. This causes winging of the scapula, which often occurs from a traction incident.

The suprascapular nerve

Compression of the suprascapular nerve associated with pain and weakness in throwing sports has been described in suprascapular nerve entrapment at the notch and with occult ganglia pressing the suprascapular nerve in the supraspinous fossa. The nerve is also susceptible to direct blows in contact sports. Compression of the suprascapular nerve at the level of the spinoglenoid notch has been reported in stretch injuries. Isolated infraspinatus palsy is a common finding in volleyball spikers and in professional baseball players. This lesion is seen with involvement of ganglia from the glenohumeral joint, from the surface of the supraspinatus fossa, and from entrapment of the nerve at the neck of the glenoid.

The suprascapular nerve originates from the upper trunk of the brachial plexus and consists of contributions from the fifth and sixth cervical root. The nerve goes into the posterior triangle of the neck, through the scapular notch where it is fixed in a fibro-osseous canal by the transverse scapular ligament. It innervates the supraspinatus muscle giving off sensory fibers to the capsular ligamentous structures of the shoulder and acromioclavicular joint. The nerve subsequently goes around the spinoglenoid portion of the scapula ending to innervate the infraspinatus muscle. The majority of entrapment neuropathies of the suprascapular nerve have been reported at the transverse scapular ligament; it can, however, be trapped as it goes around the spinoglenoid notch or from ganglia, either from the shoulder joint or from the fibrous tissue in and about the supraspinatus fossa or the glenoid neck.

Entrapment of the suprascapular nerve has been associated with traction injuries to the shoulder and with repetitive use of the shoulder as occurs in throwing sports. Activities such as weightlifting, baseball pitching, volleyball, and back packing have been implicated as a cause of this rare nerve entrapment. Trauma from crossbody adduction also has been implicated in a neurapraxia injury to the nerve. Clinically, there is the complaint of poorly localized pain in the posterior lateral aspect of the shoulder girdle. This is followed by atrophy of the supraspinatus and/or infraspinatus musculature. Eventually, there is weakness in forward flexion and external rotation of the arm at the shoulder. The diagnosis is confirmed by electromyographic and nerve-conduction studies.

Conservative therapy consists of rest, anti-inflammatory medication, and a physical therapy program designed to increase muscle tone and strength. If the conservative program is unsuccessful in relieving the symptomatology and there is functional disability, surgical decompression is indicated.

Explorations of the nerve have revealed hypertrophy of the transverse scapular ligament, anomalies of the suprascapular notch, or compression in the area of the spinoglenoid notch by a ganglion cyst or by a ganglion cyst arising from the fibrous tissue in the supraspinous fossa.

Surgical procedures have ranged from excision of the transverse scapular ligament to deepening of the suprascapular notch, and decompression of a ganglion cyst. The clinical response to surgery has varied from no improvement to full restoration of muscle bulk and power with resolution of the pain. If return of function occurs, resumption of activities can take place. If either of these muscles have not improved to at least 90 percent of full function, they inhibit the synchronous shoulder motion necessary for normal athletic function of the arm at the shoulder.

The musculocutaneous nerve

This nerve is susceptible to direct frontal blows. There is associated numbness in the lateral forearm to the base of the thumb, with a weak to absent biceps function.

Liveson (1984) reported on the electro-diagnostic examination of 11 patients with shoulder dislocation which revealed nerve damage not previously reported. Although axillary nerve lesions were the most common, posterior cord and musculocutaneous nerve damage occurred in 5 cases. The most surprising patterns of injury were associated with blunt injury or recurrent spontaneous dislocation.

Milton's report (1953) concluded that a combination of downward traction with external rotation places the musculocutaneous nerve on a stretch causing a neurapraxia.

The axillary nerve

The axillary nerve arises from the posterior cord of the brachial plexus. It contains fibers of C5 and C6 nerve roots. The nerve travels laterally and downward, passing below the shoulder joint into the quadrilateral space, curving around the posterior and lateral portion of the proximal humerus dividing into anterior and posterior bundles that innervate the deltoid and teres minor muscles. A cutaneous sensory branch supplies the lateral aspect of the upper arm.

The usual mechanism of injury to the axillary nerve is trauma either by direct blow to the posterior aspect of the shoulder or following a dislocation of the shoulder or a fracture of the proximal humerus.

Axillary nerve injury occurs in many sports such as football, wrestling, gymnastics, mountain climbing, rugby, and baseball. The degree of injury to the nerve varies since the initial presentation may be mild weakness of elevation and abduction of the arm with or without numbness in the lateral arm. Many authors have stated that 25 percent of dislocated shoulders are associated with axillary nerve-traction injuries; if electrophysical testing was utilized in all shoulder dislocations that percentage would be greater. Fortunately, traction injuries to the axillary nerve usually respond favorably to rest, time, and physical therapy. If recovery is not complete after three months, surgical intervention is recommended with exploration, utilizing neurolysis or nerve grafting. The results of these procedures are usually gratifying. Travlos et al (1990) reported on 28 patients with brachial plexus lesions caused by shoulder dislocation and stated that isolated axillary nerve lesions had the poorest prognosis for spontaneous recovery. It should be noted that the signs of neurapraxia and neurotmesis are similar. With neurapraxia, however, the nerve deficits are quite transitory. Travlos felt that there was no indication to explore until 3–5 months of time have elapsed. To wait longer than this is disadvantageous since the results of nerve repair after that period are not good.

The return of sensation may be a good indicator of potential for motor recovery. No patient who failed to obtain motor recovery had deep pressure sensation. Most of those who recovered without operation had deep pressure sensation within two months of injury. Gross sensory recovery always occurred before motor recovery.

Quadrilateral space syndrome

Quadrilateral space syndrome is involved with compression of the posterior humeral circumflex artery and the axillary nerve. This space is bounded by the teres minor superiorly, the teres major inferiorly, the humeral shaft laterally, and the long head of the triceps medially. The nerve and artery pierce the fascial plane between the teres minor and major, thus supplying the teres minor and deltoid musculature.

The patients are usually adults between the age of 22 and 35. The syndrome eventually interferes not only with their sport but also with their activities of daily living. In the athlete, it always involves a dominant extremity.

Diagnosis is difficult to make since the symptoms begin with a slow, intermittent onset of pain and paresthesias in the upper extremity, like many other shoulder complaints. Forward flexion, abduction, and external rotation such as in the throwing act accentuate the symptomatology. At times, the pain will awaken individuals at night; however, it must be noted that shoulder pain occurring at night is commonly seen in rotator cuff problems and cervical spine pathology.

Discrete point tenderness is always found posteriorly in the quadrilateral space. The maximal tenderness is almost at the insertion of the teres minor. Abduction and external rotation of the humerus for approximately one minute will often reproduce the symptomatology. There may be some difference in the quality of radial pulse in the abducted and externally rotated position. There is weakness to extension of the arm as the posterior deltoid muscle is involved. Electromyographic evaluation of the deltoid muscle has been reported as normal with involvement of the axillary nerve at the quadrilateral space; however, the author has seen this syndrome with nerve-conduction velocities slowed.

A subclavian arteriogram should be performed according to the Seldinger technique wherein dye is injected in the artery with the humerus at the side and also in abduction and external rotation. The dye must be followed distally allowing the posterior humeral circumflex artery to be visualized (*Figure 12.3*).

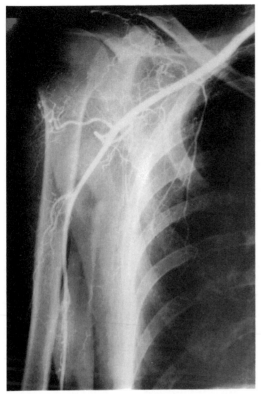

Figure 12.3

Subclavian arteriogram.

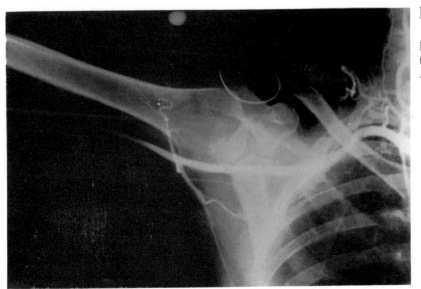

Figure 12.4

Radiograph demonstrating thoracic outlet syndrome.

In a positive arteriogram, the posterior circumflex artery may be patent with the humerus at the side and will occlude with as little as 60° of abduction; at times, however, full abduction and external rotation is necessary.

A conservative program is undertaken with avoidance of the positions of abduction and external rotation as often as possible. A graduated program of strengthening of the musculature about the shoulder must be incorporated in the overall program.

Surgical decompression of the quadrilateral space is reserved for those patients who have continued symptomatology in spite of an integrated conservative program. It is interesting to note that approximately 70 percent of patients with arteriograms that reveal occlusion of the posterior humeral circumflex artery do not have sufficient symptomatology to undergo surgical decompression.

Acute brachial neuropathy in athletes (Parsonage-Turner syndrome)

Acute brachial neuropathy has been described by a variety of names including multiple neuritis, localized neuritis of the shoulder girdle, acute brachial radiculitis, neuralgic amyopathy, shoulder girdle syndrome, viral brachial neuritis, brachial plexus neuropathy, and paralytic brachial neuritis. The pathogenesis is unknown, but proposed etiologies have included viral infection, allergy, and its association with athletic activity. This entity must therefore be included in the differential diagnosis of athletes with acute incapacitating shoulder pain.

If there is the onset of acute pain without prior contact, which is persistent, burning and involves the dominant arm, this diagnosis must be considered. Electromyography and nerve-conduction studies often confirm the diagnosis; however, these are not positive for at least 14 days following the onset of symptoms.

Pain usually resolves within a two-week period, followed by significant atrophy of the shoulder girdle musculature, particularly the supraspinatus, infraspinatus, deltoid, and serratus anterior musculature.

The prognosis for functional recovery from acute brachial neuropathy is generally good. Of patients who reported recovery, it began within the first month after the onset of weakness and was complete within three years. Tsairis et al (1972) stated that functional recovery without recurrence was apparent in 89 percent of their patients by the end of the third year. Hershman et al (1989) stated that all five of their patients were participating in sports even though there was occasional fatigue about the shoulder. There was a persistence of scapular winging in three individuals, mild proximal weakness in four individuals, and severe deltoid and external rotator weakness in one individual.

Treatment of acute brachial neuropathy can be divided into two phases. The initial period includes the time from onset of symptoms until the resolution of pain. The extremity is rested since activity is associated with increased symptomatology. Analgesics are appropriate for pain control in association with a sling for comfort. The second phase begins when the pain diminishes. Rehabilitation of the upper body and the entire upper extremity is begun in order to regain strength in the denervated muscles. It is recommended that athletes reach a plateau of at least 90 percent recovery of muscle strength before return to their sport is considered. The athlete should be warned that a permanent strength deficit may be produced by this process, particularly in the athlete who has paralysis of the serratus anterior with winging of the scapula.

Thoracic outlet syndrome

The symptomatology resulting from thoracic outlet compression is neurologic, arterial, or venous in origin. Obstruction of the subclavian vein can lead to stiffness of the limb, venous engorgement, edema, and even thrombophlebitis. Arterial symptoms may be secondary to direct obstruction and many manifest coolness, pallor, and forearm claudications (*Figure 12.4*). Telford and Mattershead (1948) believe irritation of the sympathetic nerves secondary to outlet compression can cause Raynaud's phenomenon. This is associated with worsening symptoms towards the end of prolonged activity and improvement with rest. Compression of the brachial plexus causes numbness and tingling in the upper extremity. There is weakness of the upper extremity with a complaint of a heavy feeling associated with easy tiring. The origin of pain in the extremity may not be clear since it radiates into the hand, neck, forearm, or even the chest. Pain usually centers about the inner aspect of the elbow and is most likely due to irritation of the musculocutaneous nerve. In severe cases, paresthesias and diminution of light touch are present. Multiple sites of compression may occur producing complex symptomatology.

Clinical signs of thoracic outlet compression may be elicited by mimicking the activity. Doppler examination will reveal subtle changes in arterial and venous flow. The Adson maneuver may reveal obliteration of the radial pulse; however, it must be noted that 80 percent of normal individuals demonstrate this without evidence of thoracic outlet compression.

Electromyographic and nerve-conduction velocities studies should be performed during the investigative process for this condition. Most authors agree that the nonoperative approach should be the treatment of choice, especially in the less-severe forms of thoracic outlet syndromes. Once the pain subsides, an exercise program to strengthen the suspensory musculature of the shoulder girdle is initiated. Special exercises to strengthen the upper and lower trapezius and the serratus anterior and erector spinae musculature, coupled with attention to correct the drooping shoulders, have yielded good results in most patients. An ongoing maintenance program must be performed once improvement is reached.

Progression of the symptomatology or failure of the nonoperative approach after a few months is an indication to surgical exploration and proper treatment of the observed pathology.

13

Vascular lesions about the shoulder girdle

This chapter discusses vascular lesions that occur about the shoulder girdle in the throwing athlete. These conditions are more common than previously believed: there has been an increased awareness of these problems, and more reports have been forthcoming.

The diagnosis of these conditions is not often entertained; however, when confronted with a prodrome of upper extremity fatigability and infraclavicular swelling, coupled with the catastrophic onset of swelling and cyanosis of the upper extremity, one must think of these lesions.

Arterial occlusions in the subclavian and axillary arteries

The subclavian artery may be angulated over a cervical transverse process, a cervical rib, or the first rib, or be compressed by the anterior scalene muscle. Initial symptoms vary from intermittent blanching of the hand and fingers associated with coldness, as a result of emboli from a thrombus in the subclavian artery, Raynaud's phenomenon, or a sudden catastrophic occlusion.

The evaluation of arterial occlusion includes the examination and auscultation of the supraclavicular area to detect the presence of a mass or bruit. The radial arterial pulse may be diminished or absent. The Adson test, a decreased radial pulse with the arm extended, externally rotated with the patient looking away from the involved extremity, can be utilized to reproduce symptoms. If symptoms occur with the Adson test, a lesion of the subclavian artery or brachial plexus should be suspected. Another provocative test is to have the patient raise both arms overhead and rapidly open and close the hands. If the test is positive, cramping of the hand and fingers occurs very quickly. The diagnosis is confirmed by angiography.

The treatment is usually first-rib resection. If an acute occlusion of the subclavian artery occurs, immediate surgery is indicated with first-rib resection, removal of the thrombus, and embolectomy.

Axillary artery

The axillary artery has been reported injured in shoulder dislocations, scapular neck fractures, humeral neck fractures, and clavicle fractures. This results in a diminished pulse in the extremity with or without a decrease in color and temperature loss of the extremity.

When a major vascular injury is suspected, an angiogram is mandatory. Vascular repair should be performed, along with stabilization of an unstable fracture, if present.

Effort thrombosis

Effort thrombosis is a term used to describe thrombosis of the subclavian and axillary veins. It is caused by direct injury such as noted in direct compression over the vein or following the use of a central vein monitoring device. Indirect injury is the result of repeated physical activity such as the pitching act.

The condition is a form of thoracic outlet syndrome, which accounts for less than 2 percent of all reported incidence of deep-vein thrombosis in competitive swimmers, hockey players, and runners. At the Thomas Jefferson University Hospital we have seen this problem occur on 3 occasions in professional baseball players.

Effort thrombosis has important short-term ramifications since severe disability and pulmonary embolism have been reported to occur in 12 percent of patients with subclavian vein thrombosis.

The clinical presentation of effort thrombosis is one of a prodromal complaint of swelling in the infraclavicular area associated with a deep, dull aching sensation in the shoulder. If manifest in an acute fashion, occlusion causes swelling of the extremity, engorgement of veins, and color change to the entire extremity (*Figure 13.1*). The most com-

mon symptom noted is increased swelling of the arm which responds to elevation.

Venograms demonstrate occlusion of the axillary and subclavian veins (*Figure 13.2*).

The recommended treatment of effort-induced thrombosis is usually conservative. A strict regimen of arm elevation with anticoagulation is started, in the hope that this will prevent the extension of the clot and promote recannulization of the vein. Recently, early clot dissolution with intravenous streptokinase has been utilized with success, providing the clot is less than two weeks old.

At times, chronic symptoms occur which include fatigability of the arm with recurrent swelling.

Surgical procedures have been utilized to resolve chronic complaints of swelling and fatigability of the arm. These include decompression of the costoclavicular space or a bypass of the occlusion with a vein graft extending from the external jugular to the basilic vein. On two occasions, a vascular surgeon has performed the bypass procedure on two of our patients at the Thomas Jefferson University Hospital with complete resolution of the chronic swelling and fatigue of the involved extremity. These individuals did not return to baseball as active players.

The pathophysiology of effort thrombosis remains controversial. While trauma is often involved, cases do occur without a traumatic component. During surgery for occlusive disease, a thrombus may be found; however, there are times when a thrombus is not found. When this latter phenomenon occurs, these cases have been reported to be synonymous with Paget–Schroetter syndrome; this is, however, a misnomer since that syndrome most commonly occurs in healthy, active young males, predominantly on the right side of the body, which has been used in some unusual manner.

The currently held belief is that effort thrombosis results from mechanical obstruction with or without concomitant venous thrombosis of the subclavian vein at one or

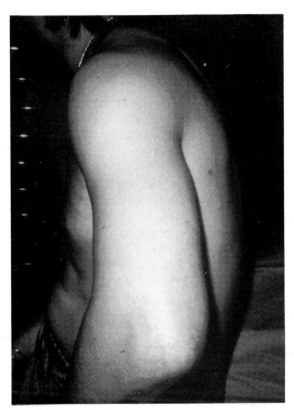

Figure 13.1

Upper extremity swelling, engorgement of veins, and color change.

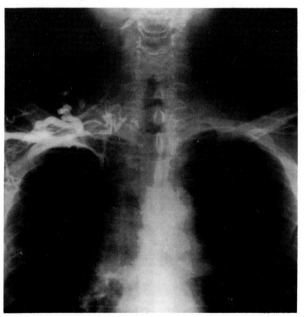

Figure 13.2

Venogram demonstrating occlusion of axillary and subclavian veins.

more points as it passes out the thoracic outlet. Wright and Lipscomb (1974) reported the onset of this problem in an 18-year-old college shortstop. He was examined eight days after a 25-game season with the main complaint of swelling and numbness of sudden onset. This symptom complex occurred the day following the cessation of playing and persisted. The swelling would decrease somewhat overnight, but with activity during the day, there would be an increase. Since the documentation by Wright and Lipscomb, a number of venous occlusions have been reported in the throwing athlete.

Nuber et al (1990) reported on vascular lesions of the shoulder in 13 athletes with symptomatology related to compression of the subclavian or axillary artery. Nine patients were minor league professional baseball pitchers who had severe arm fatigue or finger ischemia secondary to embolization as the presenting symptoms. Arteriography was performed with positional testing recreating overhead activity. Complete radiologic visualization of the dye to the digital arteries was necessary. The majority of athletes were found to have compression of the subclavian artery beneath the anterior scalene muscle, the axillary artery beneath the pectoralis minor muscle, and both arterial segments at the level of the humeral head. One pitcher occluded the posterior circumflex humeral artery with embolization to the digits.

Athletes exposed to repetitive overhead motion are at risk of upper extremity arterial compromise.

Effort thrombosis has been reported in a runner wherein the use of hand weights during aerobic exercises led to effort thrombosis. This complication should be considered when a runner complains of upper extremity muscle strain.

14

Rehabilitation of the upper extremity

Back to normal

It must be understood that the discipline of orthopaedics is concerned with the restoration of the function of the musculoskeletal system with nonsurgical methods. The treating physician has the responsibility to restore the patient to the previous environment after illness or injury. Individuals born with afflictions to the musculoskeletal system grow and develop compensatory mechanisms that enable them to function within the scope of their disability. If an individual is sound but then becomes disabled from injury or disease, the return to normal function becomes a major effort. This is particularly so in sporting activities since athletic individuals are, on many occasions, unable to cope with the problems that cause a decrease in their ability to function as an athlete or as an individual. To this end, the rehabilitation of the upper extremity in the injured athlete is now discussed.

Participation in sporting activities is extremely popular. It encompasses diverse age groups within all levels of competence, ranging from the professional to the weekend athlete. The physician who elects to treat patients with sports-related injuries must possess the necessary skills to diagnose, treat, and return individuals to full function. The rehabilitation of the athlete begins with first aid on the field and continues until the patient has returned to full activity.

The first step in the rehabilitation of an athlete begins with a preparticipation physical. This subject has for the most part been ignored, except at the higher level of team sports, college and professional. The athlete should be fully examined, including the musculoskeletal system, prior to engaging in any type of activity. The reasons are simple, since the physician is able to evaluate the patient with regard to potential problems that can occur from laxity of joints, weakness of musculature, lost joint motion, and angular deformities of the joints. With this knowledge, the important pre-athletic rehabilitation procedure must be implemented.

At the professional level of baseball, preparticipation physical examinations at a minor league level have demonstrated that a staggering 33 percent of supposed fit young men have problems related to their musculoskeletal system. Of 61 pitchers in the minor league camp, 41 had problems related to their shoulder or elbow. The most common shoulder injury was rotator cuff tendonitis with or without instability. Of those individuals with tendonitis 89 percent demonstrated X-ray changes in the area of the greater tuberosity. Sclerosis was evident in 15 percent of that group.

Plain shoulder radiographs of 58 professional pitchers were taken prior to the 1990 season with a sensitivity of 100 percent and a specificity of 27 percent in the evaluation of shoulder pathology in the elite throwing athlete. The predictive value for a positive test was 20 percent; however, a negative test had a predictive value of 100 percent. These figures suggest that X-ray evaluation of the shoulder yields little diagnostic or prognostic value. What we do not know is the long-term follow-up necessary to determine if a pitcher who had non-specific X-ray findings in 1990 will become symptomatic in 1992 or beyond. Before the institution of this radiography program, the baseball season was plagued with many instances of injury on a nonacute basis. While the acute injury can be accepted as it may be inevitable, an overuse injury should not be accepted since it is often preventable.

When an individual has started to play and then has an acute injury, the first and most important step in rehabilitation is to make an accurate and timely diagnosis of the injury. If the injury is such that surgical intervention is necessary, the operation should be performed quickly. Fortunately, many acute injuries and most overuse injuries are treated by nonoperative methods.

Initially, ice, compression with elevation of the extremity in the acute injury is utilized. Immobilization, if necessary, should be discontinued as quickly as possible since immobilization is associated with muscle atrophy. Atrophy is to be avoided at all costs, especially in the athlete. It is, therefore, important that rehabilitative exercise commence quickly. If immobilization is necessary, exercise should be performed intermittently throughout the day with the protective immobilizing device removed during that period. Isometric exercises, which are important, should be utilized in conjunction with any immobilizing device.

The injured part must be mobilized as soon as it is deemed safe. The entire human body must be involved in an exercise program that combines those exercises for strength, power, and endurance.

Since pain is a protective mechanism and must be recognized, the exercise program must be controlled and guided by the presence or absence of pain.

Swelling, an integral part of injury, must be attended to quickly. The reasoning for this is that edema, once it has become manifest, causes a significant delay in the return of the injured part to its pre-injury functional state.

A diary should be kept, with the active participation of the athlete, so that all individuals involved in the rehabilitative process can review the progression or regression of the program.

The use of isokinetic machines to exercise and test for strength, power, and endurance is an integral part of a rehabilitation program. Once the upper extremity reaches at least 90 percent of its normal strength, the athlete should be ready to commence specific athletic training, followed by competition on the field.

Greenfield et al (1990) determined isokinetic strength testing and rehabilitation be performed in the plane of the scapula. The scapular plane is defined as elevation of the shoulder in a range between 30° and 45° anterior to the frontal plane. The plane of the scapula is clinically significant because of the length–tension relationship of the shoulder abductors to its rotators. If one increases the distance from the humerus to the scapula it lengthens the rotator cuff and the deltoid musculature; therefore, the muscle-length ratio determines the amount of stretch applied to the individual sarcomeres, enabling them to exert maximum tension in this position. The length–tension curves obtained from normal muscles show that maximum tension is developed when the muscle is approximately 90 percent of its length. Conversely, when the muscle is fully shortened, the tension developed is minimal; the optimal lengthened position of the tendon apparatus will facilitate optimal muscle contraction.

Otis et al (1990) studied shoulder torque measurements from 36 normal young adult males during flexion, abduction, internal rotation, and external rotation. The effects of dominance, angular velocity, and joint position were determined. They demonstrated that only shoulder flexion exhibited significant difference with respect to dominance. In flexion torques, differences existed during isometric contractions at 0° and 90° with the dominant shoulder producing greater torque. Their study was done in young adult males and is not applicable to females, older males, and skilled athletes.

Cooper and Richards (1978) performed a similar study on 55 professional baseball players, including pitchers, wherein they demonstrated a 10 percent increase of torque of the dominant over the non-dominant upper extremity.

Werner et al (1990) determined patterns of flexibility, laxity and strength in normal shoulders, shoulders with instability, and shoulders with impingement. They concluded there are significant differences in internal rotation and external rotation ratios for peak torque and total work between nondominant and dominant shoulders of normal subjects. The dominant shoulder demonstrated significantly greater internal rotation strength when compared with the nondominant side. They found that individuals with impingement syndrome had associated posterior capsular tightness with relative weakness of the external rotators of the shoulder while individuals with anterior instability of the glenohumeral joint demonstrated excessive external rotation with relative weakness of the internal rotators. In definition of muscular imbalance patterns to differentiate between impingement and instability, it is important to distinguish between the younger and older populations as well as to attempt to separate patients in the younger population with an impingement instability complex from those with impingement or instability alone.

Cook et al (1987) investigated the shoulder-strength ratios obtained from college-level baseball pitchers and age- and sex-matched nonpitchers. Shoulder flexion, extension, and internal and external rotation-strength ratios were assessed in 10 pitchers and 9 nonpitchers. The speeds selected for testing were 180° and 300° per second on a Cybex II. The results indicated both pitchers and nonpitchers generated greater peak torque values for the extensors and internal rotators than for the flexors and external rotators of the shoulder.

Treatment protocols

Treatment protocols are described in the Appendix for review and use. They deal with:

- Impingement without surgery
- Acromioplasty alone
- Acromioplasty with rotator cuff repair
- Anterior shoulder reconstruction; and
- Instabilities of the shoulder
- Thoracic outlet syndrome

Methods of exercise performance are demonstrated (*Figure 14.1–14.47*).

At the end of a season, an off-season throwing program is encouraged and given to all of the players in the Philadelphia Phillies' organization (Table 14.1). This is a model that can and should be utilized at the high-school and higher levels of pitching. At the conclusion of that program, a protocol for the progression to pitching in a game can be utilized. These protocols are also utilized during the season if a pitcher has been injured and is getting ready to return to his previous level of proficiency.

Figure 14.1 Rowing.

Starting position: from a
standing position, bend
forward at the waist until
the upper body is close to
parallel to the floor.
Weights are held in an
extended elbow position.

Movement: Leading with
the elbow, the weight is
lifted as high as possible.

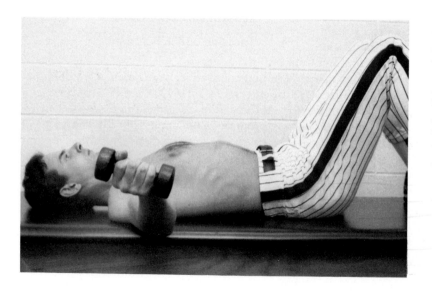

**Figure 14.2
Horizontal flexion.**

Starting position: From a
back lying position, the
arms are extended out to
the sides to the height of
the shoulders.

**Figure 14.3
Horizontal flexion.**

Movement: Weights are
lifted until they meet
centered over the chest.

Figure 14.4 Press.

Starting position: From a
back lying position, the
elbows are at the side and
flexed so weights are next
to the shoulders.

Figure 14.5 Press.

Movement: Weights are
pressed into an extended
vertical arm position.

**Figure 14.6 Straight
arm press.**

Starting position: From a
back lying position, the
arms are extended in a
vertical position.
    Movement: Weights are
pressed into an elevated
position with motion
occurring at the shoulder
(see *Figure 14.5*).

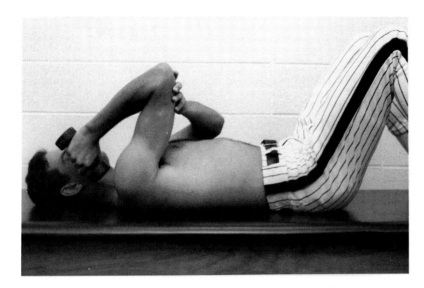

Figure 14.7 Triceps.

Starting position: From a
back lying position, the
arms are extended to the
vertical, elbows flexed.

Figure 14.8 Triceps.

Movement: Weights are
lifted to an extended
vertical arm position.

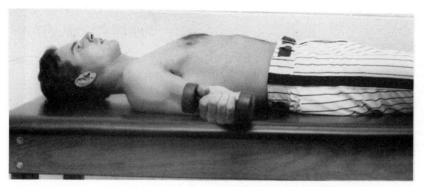

Figure 14.9 Internal rotation.

Starting position: From a back lying position, the arms are held at the side, elbows flexed and externally rotated.

Figure 14.10 Internal rotation

Movement: Weights are lifted to a vertical position.

**Figure 14.11
External rotation**

Starting position: From a
side lying position, the
elbow is flexed to 90° and
held next to the ribs.

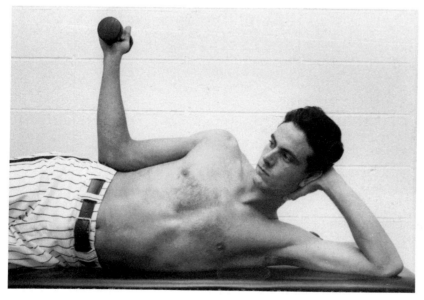

**Figure 14.12
External rotation**

Movement: Weight is lifted
from a crossbody position
to the vertical.

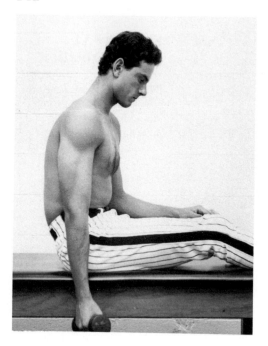

Figure 14.13 Biceps curls.

Starting position: Standing or sitting with arms
extended at sides.

Figure 14.14 Biceps curls.

Movement: Weights are lifted to shoulders by
flexing the elbows.

Figure 14.15 Wrist flexion.

Starting position: The forearms are supported with the hands facing up.

Figure 14.16 Wrist flexion.

Movement: Weights are lifted by flexing the wrist.

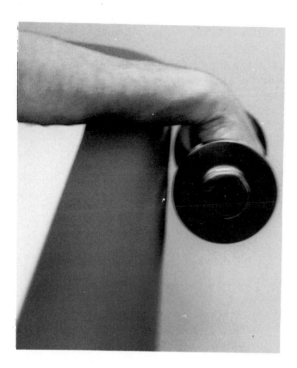

Figure 14.17 Wrist extension.

Starting position: The forearms are supported
with the hands facing down.

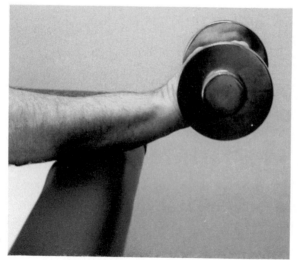

Figure 14.18 Wrist extension.

Movement: weights are lifted by extending the
wrist.

Figure 14.19 Pronation/supination.

Starting position: The forearm is supported and a
counterbalance is held in a palm-down position.

Figure 14.20 Pronation/supination.

Movement: Weight is rotated to a palm-up
position and returned.

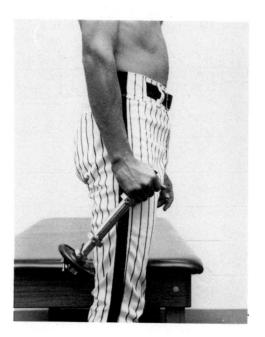

Figure 14.21 Ulnar deviation.

Starting position: Standing, a counterbalance is held with the weight extending to the rear.

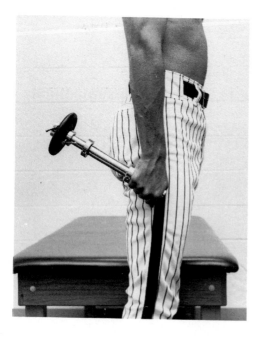

Figure 14.22 Ulnar deviation.

Movement: Weight is lifted from the lowest position toward the elbow.

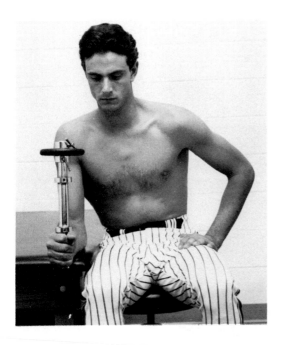

Figure 14.23 Radial deviation.

Starting position: The forearm is supported and a counterbalance is held in a thumb-up position.

Figure 14.24 Radial deviation.

Movement: Weight is lowered forward and returned toward the elbow.

Figures 14.25–14.44

Sequential passive range of motion in
conjunction with proprioceptive neurovascular
facilitation patterns.

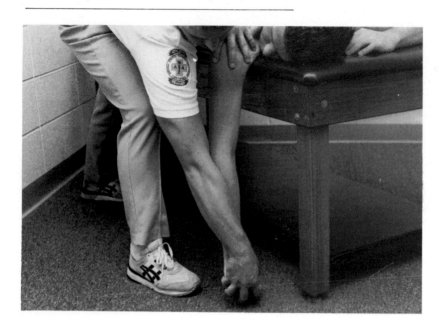

Figure 14.25

Starting position: Patient
prone with extended arm
off table and fist closed.

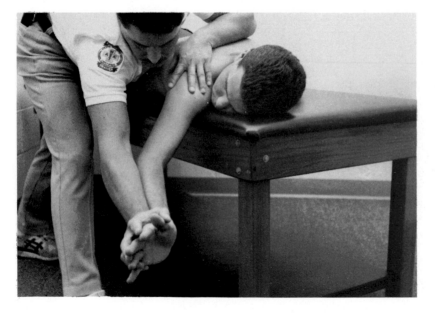

Figure 14.26

Patient raises and
externally rotates arm
while extending wrist and
fingers against resistance.

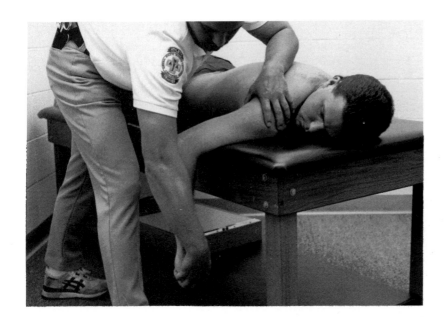

Figure 14.27

Starting position: Patient prone and shoulder abducted, arm on table with elbow off table flexed to 90° with wrist neutral and fingers flexed.

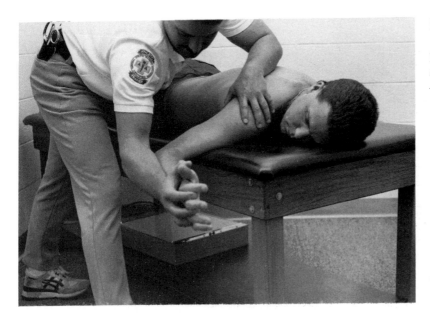

Figure 14.28

Patient externally rotates shoulder, extending fingers.

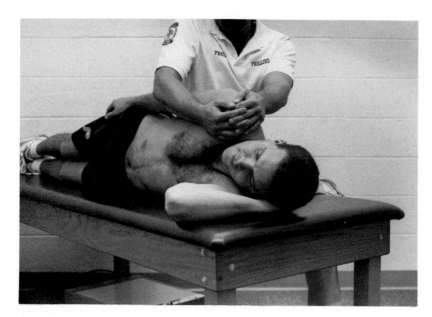

Figure 14.29

Starting position: Arm at
side with shoulder girdle
depressed.

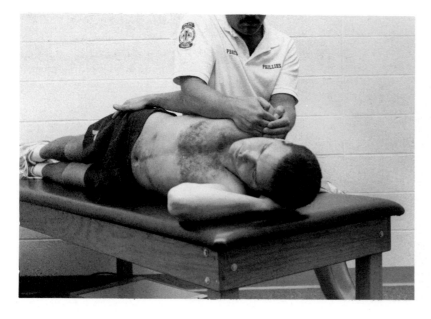

Figure 14.30

Patient elevates shoulder
girdle against resistance.

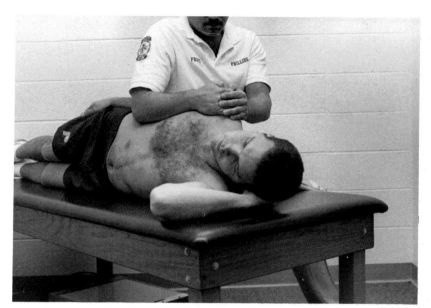

Figure 14.31

Patient continues (from *Figure 14.30*) rotating shoulder girdle superiorly and anteriorly against resistance.

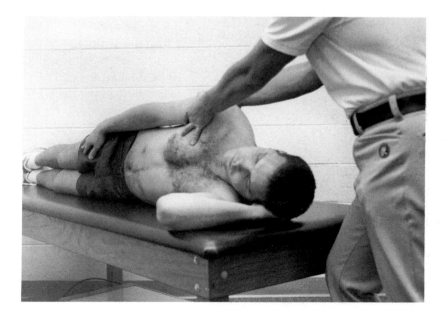

Figure 14.32

Patient elevates shoulder girdle against resistance.

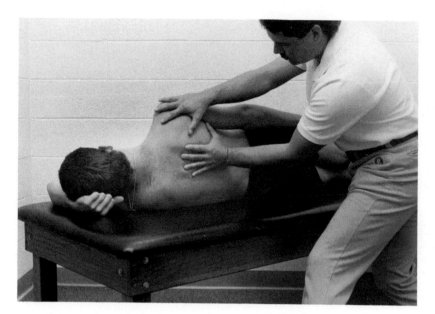

Figure 14.33

Patient depresses shoulder
girdle against resistance at
scapula.

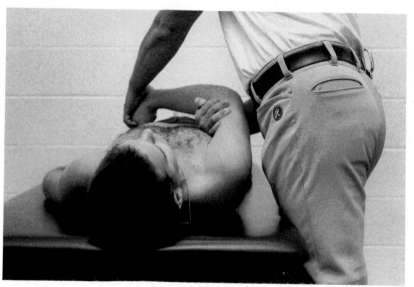

Figure 14.34

Patient supine. Wrist/
fingers flexed over
abdomen to start.

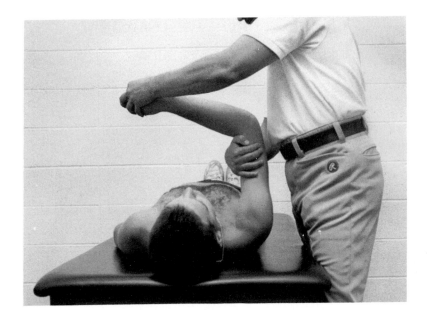

Figure 14.35

Patient flexes and externally rotates against resistance.

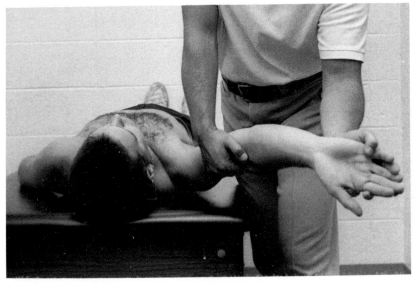

Figure 14.36

Patient continues (from *Figure 14.35*) to full shoulder abduction/external rotation extending wrist/ fingers against resistance.

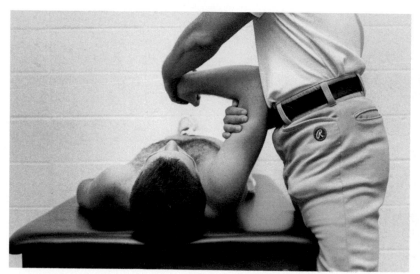

Figure 14.37

Patient supine. Shoulder forward flexed, internally rotated, elbow/wrist/fingers flexed to start.

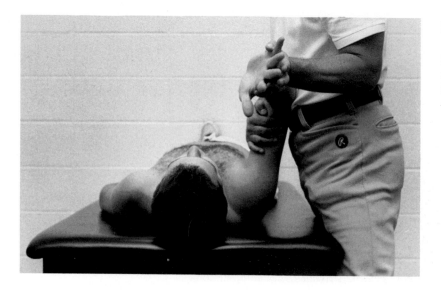

Figure 14.38

Patient externally rotates shoulder extending wrist/fingers against resistance.

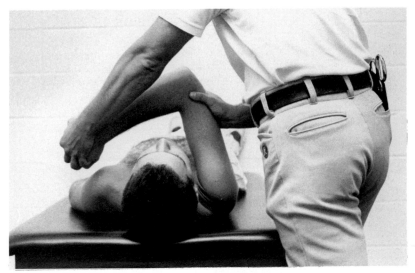

Figure 14.39

Patient supine. Shoulder
forward flexed/internally
rotated, elbow fixed, wrist
neutral, fingers flexed to
start.

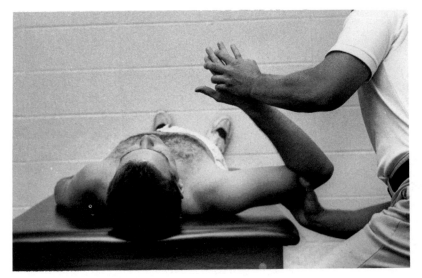

Figure 14.40

Patient abducts shoulder on
horizontal plane extending
fingers against resistance.

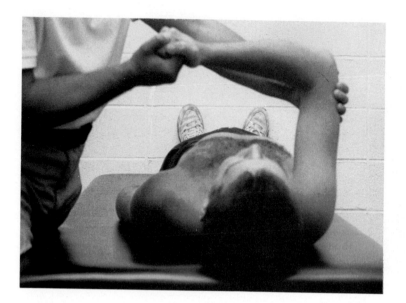

Figure 14.41

Patient supine. Shoulder
forward flexed, elbow
flexed over chest, wrist
neutral, fingers locked with
resistor to start.

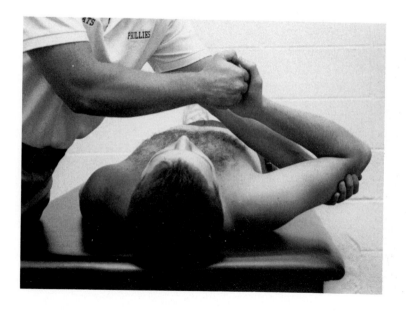

Figure 14.42

Shoulder abducted on
horizontal plane, with
elbow and fingers still
locked.

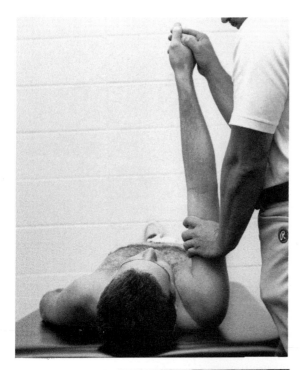

Figure 14.43

Patient supine. Shoulder forward flexed, elbow extended, wrist neutral, fingers flexed resisting depression at shoulder.

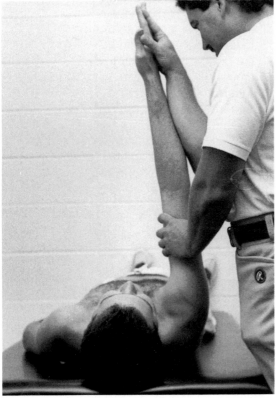

Figure 14.44

Patient supine. Shoulder forward flexed, elbow extended, wrist neutral, fingers extended, protracting shoulder girdle against resistance.

Table 14.1

Off-season throwing program.

Off-season throwing program: nine levels

1	25 warm-ups at 25 feet	25 at 60 feet	
2	25 warm-ups at 25 feet	50 at 60 feet	
3	25 warm-ups at 25 feet	75 at 60 feet	
4	25 warm-ups at 25 feet	50 at 60 feet	25 at 90 feet
5	25 warm-ups at 25 feet	50 at 60 feet	25 at 120 feet
6	25 warm-ups at 25 feet	50 at 60 feet	25 at 150 feet
7	25 warm-ups at 25 feet	50 at 60 feet	25 at 180 feet
8	25 warm-ups at 25 feet	50 at 60 feet	25 at 210 feet
9	25 warm-ups at 25 feet	50 at 60 feet	25 at 240 feet

Progression to pitching with mound work

1	25 warm-ups at 25 feet	50 mound	25 at 90 feet
2	25 warm-ups at 25 feet	60 flat	25 at 120 feet
3	25 warm-ups at 25 feet	50 mound	25 at 150 feet
4	25 warm-ups at 25 feet	60 mound	25 at 120 feet
5	25 warm-ups at 25 feet	70 flat	25 at 150 feet
6	25 warm-ups at 25 feet	60 mound	25 at 180 feet
7	25 warm-ups at 25 feet	70 mound	25 at 150 feet
8	25 warm-ups at 25 feet	60 flat	25 at 180 feet
9	25 warm-ups at 25 feet	80 mound	25 at 210 feet
10	25 premound	70 mound	25 at 240 feet
11	25 premound	80 mound	25 at 180 feet
12	25 premound	90 mound	25 at 210 feet
13	25 premound	90 mound	25 at 240 feet
14	25 premound	80 mound	25 at 180 feet
15	25 premound	100 mound	25 at 210 feet
16	25 premound	100 mound	25 at 240 feet
17	25 premound	<60 mound	
18	25 premound	100 mound	25 at 240 feet
19	25 premound	<60 mound	25 at 240 feet
20	throw batting practice	10 minutes	
21	25 premound	<60 mound	25 at 240 feet
22	throw batting practice	15 minutes	
23	25 premound	<60 mound	25 at 240 feet
24	Game: 25 premound	<60 mound warm-up	45 pitches

Appendix

Impingement

Emphasis on external rotation — also bicipital tend.

- Begin home exercise program, staying below horizontal
  1 Forward flexion/extension
  2 'Empty can' exercise described by Dr Frank Jobe isolating supraspinatus muscle – emphasis below horizontal
  3 External rotation – at 0° abduction, progressing to 90° abduction
  4 Internal rotation
  5 Prone raises — emphasis on external rotation of infraspinatus

- Start formal therapy if continued problems or stage II* at time of evaluation
  1 Modalities — ultrasound
  2 Stim
  3 Ice/heat
  4 Joint mobilization
  5 Endurance — upper body ergometer — below horizontal
  6 No bench press, military press
  7 Ice massage
  8 Progress to proprioceptive neuromuscular facilitation (PNF) — stay below horizontal and progress to full

---

* Stage II refers to degree of rotator cuff disease characterized by fibrosis and tendonitis and exhibiting pain with activity (this course is sometimes reversible).

Acromioplasty

- Presurgical instruction in range of motion (ROM) activities and isometrics
  1 ROM:
     – pendulum exercises
     – sitting pulleys for forward flexion
     – supine with cane for forward flexion
     – standing with cane for external rotation
     – standing with towel for internal rotation
     – to be performed 3–4 times a day, 5–10 repetitions
  2 Isometrics:
     – forward flexion, adduction, extension, internal and external rotation, elbow flexion and elbow extension
     – to be performed twice a day, 10 repetitions
  3 Instruct in the use of ice to the shoulder

- First post-operative visit (usually at 1 week)
  1 Review home exercise program
  2 Begin formal treatment if ROM is slow in progressing
  3 If ROM is progressing without difficulty, may begin active motion at countertop level **only**. No lifting >5 pounds

- Second post-operative visit (usually at 3–4 weeks)
  1 Review home exercise program
  2 Begin internal and external rotation strengthening
  3 Active ROM allowed: no lifting >5 pounds
  4 Begin formal therapy if ROM is slow to respond.

- Third post-operative visit (usually 7–8 weeks)
  1 Review full home exercise program
  2 Begin full strengthening program, avoiding crowding positions

- Formal treatment
  1 Modalities
  2 Joint mobilization
  3 Scapular strengthening — rhomboids, serratus
  4 ROM — corner stretches — anterior capsule
  5 PNF

Acromioplasty/rotator cuff repair

- Presurgical instruction in ROM activities and isometrics
  1 ROM
     - pendulum exercises
     - sitting pulleys for forward flexion
     - supine with cane for forward flexion
     - standing with cane for external rotation
     - standing with towel for internal rotation
     - to be performed 3–4 times a day, 5–10 repetitions
  2 Isometrics
     - forward flexion, adduction, extension, internal and external rotation, elbow flexion and elbow extension
     - to be performed twice a day, 10 repetitions
  3 Instruct in the use of ice to the shoulder

- First post-operative visit (usually at 1 week)
  1 Review home exercise program
  2 Begin formal treatment if ROM is slow in progressing

- Second post-operative visit (usually 3–4 weeks)
  1 Review full PROM program and isometrics
  2 Begin internal/external rotation strengthening
  3 Active ROM OK at countertop level; no active ROM above shoulder level
  4 IF ROM is slow to progress, begin formal treatment.

- Third post-operative visit (usually 7–8 weeks)
  1 Review full passive ROM program
  2 Add full strengthening program, avoiding crowding positions

3 If strength is slow to progress, begin formal treatment

- Formal therapy starts
  1 Decreased range of motion
  2 Increased pain

- Use weight-mobilization techniques, especially caudal glides as well as anterior/posterior and posterior/anterior
  Passive Forward flexion with scapular
  ROM stabilization
  External rotation at 0° abduction and progress to 90° abduction

- Strengthening
  Emphasis in external rotation strengthening — progress to prone raises

Anterior shoulder reconstruction

- First post-operative visit (usually 1 week post-operative)
  No physical therapy initiated.

- Second post-operative visit (usually 3–4 weeks)
  1 ROM
  - pendulum exercises
  - sitting pulleys for forward flexion
  - supine with cane for forward flexion
  - standing with cane for external rotation only to 60°
  - standing with towel for internal rotation
  - to be performed 3–4 times a day, 5–10 repetitions
  2 Instruct in the use of heat before treatment and ice following

- Third post-operative visit (usually 7–8 weeks)
  1 Full ROM activities
  2 Begin strengthening activities
  - external rotation to 60° sidelying
  - internal rotation starting from neutral sidelying

- Fourth post-operative visit (usually 10–12 weeks)
  1 Full strengthening program
  2 Begin formal therapy if strength is slow to progress

- Modalities in formal treatment
  1 Contrast early
  2 Stim

Instabilities

Anterior

- Emphasis on internal rotation
- Total shoulder work
- Training to prevent excessive abduction and external rotation in activities of daily living
- Formal treatment
  1 Modalities
  2 PNF
  3 Biodex

Posterior

- Emphasis on external rotation
- External rotation side program
- Prone raises
- Total shoulder work

Thoracic outlet syndrome exercises

Do each activity 6 times, 5 times daily (Peet et al 1956; Smith 1979).

1 Stand erect with arms at sides: shrug shoulders forward and upward – relax – and then backwards and upward – relax – and then straight upwards. **Do this slowly and smoothly**

2 Stand erect with arms at sides: raise arms out to the side and up until hands meet above the head with elbows straight

3 Stand facing a corner of a room with one hand on each wall, arms at shoulder level, palms forward, elbows bent: slowly lean upper body into wall and then press back out

4 Stand erect with arms at sides: bend head to the left, trying to touch ear to shoulder, without shrugging shoulders. Repeat to the right

5 Lie face down with arms bent at sides: raise arms, head, and chest in air, pulling shoulders back and keeping chin tucked – **hold** in air for 3 seconds. Inhale as chest is raised and exhale as you lower yourself

6 Lie down on back with towel roll between shoulder blades (no pillow under the head): inhale and raise arms above head and back. Exhale as you lower arms

7 Lie face down: move arms from behind low back, then out to the side and then overhead

8 Lie face down with hand and arm over the edge of the bed: raise up arm with elbow bent and 5 lb weight in hand

9 Stand erect with arms at sides: turn head over to left shoulder and then to right shoulder

10 Stand erect with face straight ahead: tuck chin

Things to avoid

1 Avoid activities that result in prolonged overhead extension of arms
2 If necessary, hold arm in a pocket or belt loop when walking
3 When sitting, support arm on a armrest or on a pillow
4 When driving, hold the steering wheel at the bottom – not at the top
5 Wearing heavy coats, overalls, or restrictive clothing can only further aggravate the problem
6 Large, heavy purses further stretch the shoulders. Also, avoid backpacks, golf-bags, briefcases and suitcases (on the involved side)
7 When sleeping, avoid putting arms under a pillow or overhead. It is recommended that you keep one pillow under head, one under shoulder and one under that side right next to spine
8 If an acute episode occurs in public, roll shoulders a few times, straighten upper back, and place hand in coat pocket or into belt or waistband. Relax arm

References

Adams JE (1968), Bone injuries in very young athletes, *Clin Orthop* **58**: 129.

Adams JT, DeWeese JA (1971), Effort thrombosis of the axillary and subclavian veins, *J Trauma* **11**: 923.

Alexander OM (1954), Radiography of the acromioclavicular articulation, *Medical Radiography and Photography (England)* **30**: 34–9.

Allman F (1967), Fractures and ligamentous injuries of the clavicle and its articulation, *J Bone Joint Surg (Am)* **49**: 774–84.

Allman FL (1978), Report of more than 300 Bristow Procedures of the shoulder, *J Bone Joint Surg (Am)* **33**: 261.

Altchek DW, Warren RF, Wickiewicz TL et al (1990), Arthroscopic acromioplasty: technique and results, *J Bone Joint Surg (Am)* **72**: 1198–1207.

American Academy of Orthopaedic Surgeons (1962), *The measuring and recording of joint motion.*

Anderson IE, Ciolek J (1989), Specific rehabilitation programs for the throwing athlete, *Sports Med* **46**: 487–91.

Andrews JR, Carson WG, Ortega K (1984), Arthroscopy of the shoulder: technique and normal anatomy, *Am J Sports Med* **12**: 1–7.

Apple DF, O'Toole J, Annis C (1982), Professional basketball injuries, *Phys Sports Med* **10**: 81.

Armstrong CP, Van der Spuy DR (1984), The fractured scapula: importance and management based on a series of 62 patients, *Injury* **15**: 324–9.

Barnes DA, Tullos HS (1978), An analysis of 100 symptomatic baseball players, *Am J Sports Med* **6**: 62–7.

Basmajian JV, Bazant FJ (1959), Factors preventing downward dislocation of the shoulder joint: an electromyographic and morphological study, *J Bone Joint Surg (Am)* **41**: 1182–6.

Bateman JE (1967), Nerve injuries about the shoulder in sports, *J Bone Joint Surg (Am)* **49**: 785.

Becker GJ, Holden RW, Rabe FE (1983), Local thrombolytic therapy for subclavian and axillary vein thrombosis, *Radiology* **149**: 419.

Benchetrit E, Friedman B (1977), Fracture of the coracoid process associated with subglenoid dislocation of the shoulder, *J Bone Joint Surg (Am)* **61**: 295–6.

Benton J, Nelson C (1971), Avulsion of the coracoid process in an athlete, *J Bone Joint Surg (Am)* **53**: 356–8.

Berry H, Bril V (1982), Axillary nerve palsy following blunt trauma to the shoulder region. A clinical and electrophysical review, *J Neurol Neurosurg Psychiatry* **45**: 1027–32.

Biener K, Muller P, Ice hockey accidents, unpublished data.

Bigliani LU, Flatow EL, Deliz ED (1991), Complications of shoulder arthroscopy, *Orthop Rev* **20**: 743–51.

Bigliani LU, Morrison DS, April EW (1986), Morphology of the acromion and its relationship to rotator cuff tears, *Orthop Trans* **10**: 459.

Birrer RB, Birrer CD (1982), Martial arts injuries, *Phys Sports Med* **10**: 103.

Boehme D, Curtis RJ, DeHaan JT et al (1991), Non-union of fractures of the mid-shaft of the clavicle, *J Bone Joint Surg (Am)* **73**: 1219–26.

Booth CM, Roper BA (1979), Chronic dislocation of the sternoclavicular joint, *Clin Orthop* **140**: 17–20.

Bosley RC (1991), Total arthroscopy: a twenty year review, *J Bone Joint Surg (Am)* **73**: 961–8.

Boyer DW (1975), Trapshooter's shoulder: stress fracture of the coracoid process, *J Bone Joint Surg (Am)* **57**: 862.

Bracker MD, Cohen M, Blasingame J (1990), Chronic shoulder pain in volleyball players, *Phys Sports Med* **18**: 85–8.

Brady TA, Cahill BR, Bodnar IM (1982), Weight training related injuries in the high school athlete, *Am J Sports Med* **10**: 1.

Brandt TD, Cardone BW, Grant TH et al (1989), Rotator cuff sonography: a reassessment, *Radiology* **173**: 323–7.

Brunet ME, Reynolds MC, Cook SD et al (1986), Atraumatic osteolysis of the distal clavicle: histologic evidence of synovial pathogenesis, *Orthopedics* **9**: 557–9.

Bryan AS, Klenerman L, Bowsher D (1991), The diagnosis of reflex sympathetic dystrophy, *J Bone Joint Surg (Br)* **73**: 644–6.

Buckley P, Grana WA (1990), When does a sore shoulder signal an injured rotator cuff? *Your Patient and Fitness* **6**: 5–9.

Burk DL Jr, Karasick D, Kurtz AB et al (1989), Rotator cuff tears: prospective comparison of MR imaging with arthrography, sonography, and surgery, *AJR* **153**: 87–92.

Burk DL Jr, Karasick D, Mitchell DG et al (1990), MR imaging of the shoulder: correlation with plain radiography, *AJR* **154**: 549–53.

Burk DL Jr, Torres JL, Marone PJ et al (1991), MR imaging of shoulder injuries in professional baseball players, *JMRI* **1**: 385–9.

Burroughs P, Dahners CE (1990), The effect of enforced exercise on the healing of ligament injuries, *Am J Sports Med* **18**: 376–8.

Cahill BR (1982), Osteolysis of the distal part of the clavicle in male athletes, *J Bone Joint Surg (Am)* **64**: 1053–8.

Cahill BR, Palmer PE (1983), Quadrilateral space syndrome, *J Hand Surg* **8**: 65.

Cahill BR, Tullos HS, Fain RH (1974), Little league shoulder, *J Sports Med* **2**: 150.

Clein LJ (1975), Suprascapular entrapment neuropathy, *J Neurosurg* **43**: 337.

Cofield RH (1987), Managing rotator cuff tears, instructional course lecture, AAOS.

Cook EE, Gray VL, Savinar-Nogue E et al (1987), Shoulder antagonistic strength ratios: a comparison between college level baseball pitchers and non-pitchers, *J Orthop Sports Phys Ther* **8**: 451–5.

Cook DA, Heiner JR (1990), Acromioclavicular joint injuries, *Orthop Rev* **19**: 511–16.

Cooper JF, Richards JR (1978), Dominant to non-dominant eccentric rotator cuff strength in professional baseball pitchers, unpublished data.

Cox JS (1981), The fate of the acromioclavicular joint in athletic injuries, *Am J Sports Med* **9**: 50–3.

Cox JS (1991), Current methods of treatment of acromioclavicular joint injuries, *Jefferson Orthopaedic J* 56–9.

Cunningham's manual of practical anatomy, 11th edn (1949), (Oxford, Oxford University Press).

Daluga DJ, Quast M, Bach BR et al (1990), Shoulder neoplasms mimicking rotator cuff tears, *Orthopaedics* **13**: 765–7.

DePalma AF (1983), *Surgery of the shoulder*, 3rd edn (JB Lippincott, Philadelphia).

DeRosa GP, Kettlekamp DB (1977), Fracture of the coracoid process of the scapula, *J Bone Joint Surg (Am)* **59**: 696–7.

DiBenedetto M, Markey K (1984), Electrodiagnostic localization of traumatic upper trunk brachial plexopathy, *Archives Physical Med and Rehab* **65**: 15–17.

Drez SP (1976), Suprascapular neuropathy in the differential diagnosis of rotator cuff injuries, *Am J Sports Med* **4/2**: 43.

Dyro FM (1983), Peripheral entrapments following brachial plexus lesions, *Electromyogr Clin Neurophysiol* **23**: 251–6.

Ellenbecker TS, Derscheid GL (1989), Rehabilitation of overuse injuries of the shoulder, *Clin Sports Med* **8**: 583–603.

Ellman H (1987), Arthroscopic subacromial decompression: analysis of one–three year results, *Arthroscopy* **3**: 173–81.

Esch JC (1989), Arthroscopic subacromial decompression: surgical technique, *Orthop Rev* **18**: 6.

Estwanik JJ (1989), Levator scapulae syndrome, *Phys Sports Med* **7**: 57–68.

Ferrari DA (1990), Capsular ligaments of the shoulder: anatomical and functional study of the anterior superior capsule, *Am J Sports Med* **18**: 20–4.

Ferretti A, Cerullo G, Russo G (1987), Suprascapular neuropathy in volleyball players, *J Bone Joint Surg (Br)* **69**: 260.

Flatow EL, Cuomo P, Maday MG et al (1991), Open reduction and internal fixation of two-part displaced fractures of the greater tuberosity of the proximal part of the humerus, *J Bone Joint Surg (Am)* **73**: 1213–18.

Fowler P (1983), Shoulder pain in highly competitive swimmers, *Orthop Trans* **7**: 170.

Fukada H (1987), Surgical treatment of incomplete thickness tears of rotator cuff: long term follow-up, course lecture, AAOS.

Fukuda K, Craig EV, An KN et al (1986), Biomechanical study of the ligamentous system of the acromioclavicular joint, *J Bone Joint Surg (Am)* **68**: 434–9.

Fullerton LR (1990), Recurrent third degree acromioclavicular joint separation after failure of a Dacron ligament prosthesis, *Am J Sports Med* **18**: 106–7.

Ganzhorn RW et al (1981), Suprascapular nerve entrapment, *J Bone Surg* **63**: 492.

Gartsman GM (1988), Arthroscopic subacromial decompression for Stage III impingement: the first 100 cases, *Orthop Trans* **12**: 672.

Goldberg BP, Vicks B (1983), Oblique angled view for coracoid fractures, *Skeletal Radiology* **9**: 195–7.

Gonzalez D, Lopez RA (1991), Concurrent rotator cuff tear and brachial plexus palsy associated with anterior dislocation of the shoulder, *J Bone Joint Surg (Am)* **73**: 620–1.

Greenfield BH, Donatelli R, Wooden MJ et al (1990), Isokinetic evaluation of shoulder rotational strength between the plane of the scapula and the frontal plane, *Am J Sports Med* **18**: 124–8.

Gross ML, Seeger LL, Smith JB et al (1990), Magnetic resonance imaging of the glenoid labrum, *Am J Sports Med* **18**: 229–34.

Haber EC, Storey MD (1990), Effort thrombosis in a runner, *Phys Sports Med* **18**: 76–84.

Hadley MN (1986), Suprascapular nerve entrapment, *J Neurosurg* **64**: 843.

Harding W, Starr L (1990), Analysis of pain in the throwing shoulder, *PBATS Newsletter* **3/1**: 1–2.

Harryman DT II, Mack LA, Wang KY et al (1991), Repairs of the rotator cuff: correlation of functional results with integrity of the cuff, *J Bone Joint Surg (Am)* **73**: 982–9.

Hawkins RJ (1980), The acromioclavicular joint, paper presented at the AAOS Summer Institute.

Hawkins RJ, Brock RM, Abrams JS et al (1988), Acromioplasty for impingement with an intact rotator cuff, *J Bone Joint Surg (Br)* **70**: 795–7.

Hawkins RJ, Kennedy JC (1980), Impingement syndrome in athletes, *Am J Sports Med* **8**: 151.

Henry JH, Lareau B, Neigut D (1982), The injury rate in professional basketball, *Am J Sports Med* **10**: 16.

Hershman EB, Wilburn AJ, Bergfeld JP (1989), Acute brachial neuropathy in athletes, *Am J Sports Med* **17**: 655–9.

Heyse-Moore GH, Stoker DJ (1982), Avulsion fractures of the scapula, *Skeletal Radiology* **9**: 27–32.

Hirayama T, Takemitsu Y (1981), Compression of the suprascapular nerve by ganglion at the suprascapular notch, *Clin Orthop* **155**: 95.

Hitchcock HH, Bechtol CO (1948), Painful shoulder, *J Bone Joint Surg (Am)* **30**: 267.

Ho WP, Chen JY, Shih CH (1988), The surgical treatment of complete acromioclavicular joint dislocation, *Orthop Rev* **17**: 1116–20.

Horwitz BR, Fenlin JM, Bartolozzi AR et al (1989), Correlation of MRI and arthrography with surgical findings in rotator cuff disease, abstract study, Department of Orthopaedic Surgery/Department of Radiology, Thomas Jefferson University, Philadelphia.

Hovelius L (1978), Shoulder dislocation in Swedish ice hockey players, *Am J Sports Med* **6**: 373–7.

Howell SM, Galinat BJ (1987), The containment mechanism: the primary stabilizer of the glenohumeral joint, paper presented at AAOS Annual Meeting.

Hurley JA, Anderson TE (1990), Shoulder arthroscopy: its role in evaluating shoulder disorders in the athlete, *Am J Sports Med* **18**: 480–3.

Imatani RJ, Hanlon JJ, Cady GW (1975), Acute complete acromioclavicular joint dislocations, *J Bone Joint Surg (Am)* **57**: 328.

Inman VT, Saunders JBDeCM, Abbott LeRC (1944), Observations on the function of the shoulder joint, *J Bone Joint Surg* **26**: 3–32.

Jobe FW, Bradley JP, Pink M (1990), Impingement syndrome in overhand athletes I, *Surgical Rounds for Orthopaedics* 21.

Jobe FW, Giangarra CE, Kvitne RS et al (1991), Anterior capsulolabral reconstruction of the shoulder in athletes in overhand sports, *Am J Sports Med* **19**: 428–34.

Jobe FW, Kvitne RS (1989), Shoulder pain in the overhand or throwing athlete, *Orthop Rev* **18**: 963–75.

Jobe FW, Moynes DR, Tibone JE et al (1984), An EMG analysis of the shoulder in pitching: a second report, *Am J Sports Med* **12**: 218–20.

Jobe FW, Tibone JE, Perry J et al (1983), An EMG analysis of the shoulder in throwing and pitching: a preliminary report, *Am J Sports Med* **11**: 3–5.

Jordan BD, Istrico R, Zimmerman RD et al (1990), Acute cervical radiculopathy in weight lifters, *Phys Sports Med* **18**: 1.

Jupiter J (1989), Non-union of the clavicle, *Complications in Orthopaedics* Jan/Feb: 29–32.

Kaplan J (1983), Electromyography and nerve conduction velocities, *Current Concepts in Pain* **1/5**: 11–16.

Karzel R (1990), MRI remains less reliable than arthroscopy for shoulder diagnoses, but gadolinium helps, *Orthopaedics Today* Nov: 20.

Kazar B, Relovszky E (1969), Prognosis of primary dislocations of the shoulder, *Acta Orthop Scand* **40**: 216.

Kennedy JC, Hawkins RJ (1974), Swimmer's shoulder, *Phys Sports Med* **2**: 35–8.

Kennedy JC, Hawkins RJ, Krissof WB (1978), Orthopaedic manifestations of swimming, *Am J Sports Med* **6**: 309.

Kimball RJ, Carter RL, Schneider RC (1985), Competitive diving injuries. In: Schneider RC, Kennedy JC, Plant ML, eds, *Sports injuries: mechanisms, prevention and treatment* (Baltimore, Williams and Wilkins).

Klemp P, Learmonth ID (1984), Hypermobility and injuries in a professional ballet company, *Br J Sports Med* **18**: 143.

Kuhlman JE, Fishman EK, Ney DR et al (1988), Complex shoulder trauma: three dimensional CT imaging, *Orthopaedics* **11**: 1561–3.

Kuhlman JE, Fishman EK, Ney DR et al (1989), Two and three dimensional imaging of the painful shoulder, *Orthop Rev* **18**: 1201–8.

Kumar A (1990), Management of coracoid process fracture with acromioclavicular joint dislocation, *Orthopaedics* **13**: 770–2.

Lancaster S, Horowitz M, Alonso J (1987), Complete acromioclavicular separations, *Clin Orthop* **216**: 80–7.

Lawrence WS (1918), A method of obtaining an accurate lateral roentgenogram of the shoulder joint, *AJR* **5**: 193.

Levine AH, Pais MJ, Schwartz EE (1976), Post-traumatic osteolysis of the distal clavicle with emphasis on early radiologic change, *AJR* **127**: 781–4.

Linn RM, Krieghauser LA (1991), Ball thrower's fracture of the humerus, *Am J Sports Med* **19**: 194–7.

Liveson JA (1984), Nerve lesions associated with shoulder dislocation: an electro-diagnostic study of 11 cases, *J Neurol Neurosurg Psychiatry* **47**: 742–4.

MacDonald DB, Alexander MJ, Frejuk J et al (1985), Comprehensive functional analysis of shoulders following complete acromioclavicular separation, *Am J Sports Med* **16**: 475–80.

Madsen B (1963), Osteolysis of the acromial end of the clavicle following trauma, *Br J Radiol* **36**: 822.

Mariani PP (1980), Isolated fracture of the coracoid process in an athlete, *Am J Sports Med* **8**: 129–30.

Marks J (1956), Anticoagulation therapy in idiopathic occlusion of the axillary vein, *Br Med J* **1**: 11.

Marone PJ (1987), Diagnosis and management of rotator cuff disease, Forum Medicus, Course II, Lesson IX.

Marone PJ (1986), The shoulder in throwing sports: an overview, Forum Medicus, Course I, Lesson VII.

Marone PJ, Zoller J, Stecyk ND et al (1987), Stress fracture, coracoid process. Case report, *Jefferson Orthopaedic J* **16**: 73.

Matheson GO, Clement DB, McKenzie DC et al (1987), Stress fractures in athletes, *Am J Sports Med* **12**: 46–57.

McCarroll JR (1986), Golf: common injuries from a supposedly benign activity, *J Musculoskeletal Med* **3**: 9.

McCarroll JR, Gioe TT (1982), Professional golfers and the price they pay, *Phy Sports Med* **10**: 64.

McLatchie G (1983), Karate and karate injuries, *Br J Sports Med* **17**: 131.

McLatchie GR, Davies JE, Caulley JH (1980), Injuries in karate: a case for medical control, *J Trauma* **20**: 956.

McLaughlin HL, MacLellan D (1967), Recurrent anterior dislocation of the shoulder II: a comparative study, *J Trauma* **7**: 191.

McLeod WD (1985), The pitching mechanism. In: Zarins B, Andrews JR, Carson W, eds, *Injuries to the throwing arm* (Philadelphia, WB Saunders).

Mestdagh H, Drizenko A, Ghestem P (1981), Anatomical basis of suprascapular nerve by ganglion at the suprascapular nerve syndrome, *Anatomia Clinica* **3**: 67–71.

Middleton WD (1989), Status of rotator cuff sonography, *Radiology* **173**: 307–9.

Milton GW (1953), The mechanism of circumflex and other nerve injuries in dislocation of the shoulder and the possible mechanism of nerve injuries during reduction of dislocation, *Aust NZ J Surg* **23**: 25–30.

Mogan JV, Davis PH (1982), Upper extremity injuries in skiing, *Clin Sports Med* **1**: 295.

Montgomery SP, Loyd RD (1977), Avulsion fracture of the coracoid epiphysis with acromioclavicular separation, *J Bone Joint Surg (Am)* **59**: 963–5.

Morgan CD (1989), Arthroscopic Bankart suture repair: 2 to 5 year result, *Orthop Trans* **13**: 231–2.

Morgan CD, Boderstab AB (1987), Arthroscopic Bankart suture repair: technique and early results, *Arthroscopy* **3/2**: 111–22.

Morrison DS, Bigliani LU (1987), Roentgenographic analysis of acromial morphology and its relationship to rotator cuff tears, *Orthop Trans* **11**: 439.

Morrison DS, Ofstein R (1990), The use of magnetic resonance imaging in the diagnosis of rotator cuff tears, *Orthopaedics* **13**: 633–6.

Neer CS II (1968), Fractures of the distal third of the clavicle, *Clin Orthop* **58**: 43.

Neer CS II (1987), Treatment of rotator cuff tears, AAOS course lecture.

Neer CS II, Foster CR (1980), Inferior capsular shift for involuntary, inferior and multidirectional instability of the shoulder, *J Bone Joint Surg (Am)* **62**: 897.

Neer CS II, Horwicz BS (1965), Fractures of the proximal humeral epiphyseal plate, *Clin Orthop* **41**: 24.

Neer CS II, Welsh RP (1977), The shoulder in sports, *Orthop Clin North Am* **8/3**: 583–91.

Nelson MC, Leather GP, Nirschl RP et al (1991), Evaluation of the painful shoulder: a prospective comparison of magnetic resonance imaging and operative findings, *J Bone Joint Surg (Am)* **73**: 707–16.

Nemmers DW, Thrope PE, Knibbe MA et al (1990), Upper extremity venous thrombosis, *Orthop Rev* **18**: 164–72.

Nirschl RP (1987), Rotator cuff tendonitis: basic concepts in pathoetiology, instructional course lecture, AAOS.

Noah J, Gidumal R (1988), Rotator cuff injuries in the throwing athlete, *Orthop Rev* **17**: 1091–6.

Norfray JF, Tremaine MJ, Groves HC et al (1977), The clavicle in hockey, *Am J Sports Med* **5**: 275.

Nuber GW, McCarthy WJ, Yao JST et al (1990), Arterial abnormalities of the shoulder in athletes, *Am J Sports Med* **18**: 514–19.

Ogilvie-Harris DJ (1987), Arthroscopy and arthroscopic surgery of the shoulder, *Semin Orthop* **2**: 246–58.

Ogilvie-Harris DJ, Wiley AM, Sattarian J (1990), Failed acromioplasty for impingement syndrome, *J Bone Joint Surg (Br)* **72**: 1070–2.

Olive RJ Jr (1990), Ultrasound may be best screen for rotator cuff tears, *Orthop Today* **10**: 1, 10–11.

O'Neill DB, Zarins B, Gelberman RH et al (1990), Compression of the anterior interosseous nerve after use of a sling for dislocation of the acromioclavicular joint, *J Bone Joint Surg (Am)* **72**: 1100–2.

Otis JC, Warren RF, Backus SI et al (1990), Torque production of the shoulder of the normal young adult male, *Am J Sports Med* **18**: 119–23.

Palmer I, Widen A (1948), The bone block method for recurrent dislocations of the shoulder joint, *J Bone Joint Surg (Br)* **30**: 53.

Pappas Am, Zawacki RM, McCarthy CF (1985a), Biomechanics of baseball pitching, *Am J Sports Med* **13**: 216–22.

Pappas AM, Zawacki RM, McCarthy CF (1985b), Rehabilitation of the pitching shoulder, *Am J Sports Med* **13**: 223–35.

Parker RD, Berkowitz MS, Brahams MA et al (1986), Hook of the hamate fractures in athletes, *Am J Sports Med* **14**: 517–23.

Paulos LE, Franklin JL (1990), Arthroscopic shoulder decompression development and application: a five year experience, *Am J Sports Med* **18**: 3.

Peet RM, Henriksen JD, Anderson TP et al (1956), Thoracic outlet syndrome, *Mayo Clin Proc* **81**: 281.

Penny JN, Walsh RP (1981), Shoulder impingement syndromes in athletes and their surgical management, *Am J Sports Med* **9**: 11.

Perry J (1983), Anatomy and biomechanics of the shoulder in throwing, swimming, gymnastics, and tennis, *Clin Sports Med* **2**: 247–70.

Petrucci FS, Morelli A, Raimondi PL (1982), Axillary nerve injuries: 21 cases treated by nerve graft and neurolysis, *J Hand Surg* **7**: 271.

Pink M, Jobe FW, Perry J (1990), Electromyographic analysis of the clavicle in male athletes, *Am J Sports Med* **18**: 137–40.

Post M (1955), Current concepts in the diagnosis and management of acromioclavicular dislocations, *Clin Orthop* **200**: 234–47.

Rathburn JB, Macnas I (1970), The microvascular pattern of the rotator cuff, *J Bone Joint Surg (Br)* **52**: 540–53.

Richardson AB, Jobe FW, Collins HR (1980), The shoulder in competitive swimming, *Am J Sports Med* **8**: 159.

Rockwood CA (1987), The diagnosis and indications for surgery of ruptures of the rotator cuff, instructional course lecture, AAOS.

Rockwood CA, Green DP (1984), *Fractures in adults*, 2nd edn (Philadelphia, JB Lippincott).

Rockwood CA, Imatani RJ (1975), Acute complete acromioclavicular injury, *J Bone Joint Surg (Am)* **57**: 328.

Rollins J, Puffer JC, Whiting WC et al (1985), Water polo injuries to the upper extremity. In: Zarins B, Andrews JR, Carson W, eds, *Injuries to the throwing arm* (Philadelphia, WB Saunders).

Rothman RH, Parke WW (1965), The vascular anatomy of the rotator cuff, *Clin Orthop* **41**: 176.

Rouse L, Burkhead WZ (1989), Rotator cuff debridement, *Orthop Consult* **10**: 1–12.

Rowe CR (1958), Shoulder girdle injuries. In: Cave EF, ed, *Fractures and other injuries* (Chicago, Year Book).

Rowe CR (1968), An atlas of anatomy and treatment of midclavicular fractures, *Clin Orthop* **58**: 29–42.

Rowe CR, ed (1988), *The shoulder* (Churchill Livingstone, Edinburgh).

Rowe CR, Patel D, Southmayd WW (1978), The Bankart procedure. A long term end-result study, *J Bone Joint Surg (Am)* **60**: 1–16.

Rowe CR, Sakellarides HT (1961), Factors related to recurrences of anterior dislocation of the shoulder, *Clin Orthop* 20.

Ruhl J, Protocol for acromioplasty rehabilitation developed for the Jefferson Sports Medicine Center, unpublished data.

Ruhl J, Protocol for treatment, initial and ongoing, developed for the Jefferson Sports Medicine Center, unpublished data.

Sandrock AR (1975a), Stress fracture of the coracoid process of the scapula, *Radiology* **117**: 274.

Sandrock (1975b), Another sports fatigue fracture, *Radiology* **117**: 275.

Schenkman M, Cartaya VRD (1987), Kinesiology of the shoulder complex, *J Orthop Sports Med* **8**: 438–50.

Seldinger SI (1953), Catheter placement of a needle in percutaneous arteriography. A new technique, *Acta Radiol* **39**: 368.

Shields CL, Zomar VD (1982), Analysis of professional football injuries, *Cont Orthop* **4**: 90.

Silvij S, Nocini S (1982), Clinical and radiological aspects of gymnast's shoulder, *J Sports Med* **2**: 49.

Smith KF (1979), The thoracic outlet syndrome: a protocol of treatment, *J Orthop Sports Phys Ther* **1**: 88–99.

Smith MJ, Stewart MJ (1979), Acute acromioclavicular separations, *Am J Sports Med* **7**: 62–71.

Snook GA (1979), Injuries in women's gymnastics, *Am J Sports Med* **7**: 242.

Soble MG, Kaye AD, Guay RC (1989), Rotator cuff tear: clinical experience with sonographic detection, *Radiology* **173**: 319–21.

Speer KP, Bassett FH III (1990), The prolonged burner syndrome, *Am J Sports Med* **18**: 591–4.

Stricevic MV, Patel MR, Okazaki T et al (1983), Karate: historical perspective and injuries sustained in national and international tournament competitions, *Am J Sports Med* **11**: 320.

Strickler TS, Malone T, Garrett WE (1990), The effects of passive warming on muscle injury, *Am J Sports Med* **18**: 141–5.

Strohm BR, Colachis SC Jr (1965), Shoulder joint dysfunction following injury to the suprascapular nerve, *Phys Ther* **45**: 106.

Sutherland GW (1976), Ice on fire, *Am J Sports Med* **4**: 264.

Taft TN, Wilson FC, Oglesby JW (1987), Dislocation of the acromioclavicular joint, *J Bone Joint Surg (Am)* **69**: 1945–51.

Tapper EM (1979), Ski injuries from 1939 to 1976: the Sun Valley experience, *Am J Sports Med* **7**: 114.

Telford ED, Mattershead S (1948), Pressure at the cervico-brachial junction, *J Bone Joint Surg (Br)* **30**: 249–65.

Thompson JS (1990), ORIF uniquely suited to displaced midthird clavicle fracture, paper presented at Fourth International Conference on Surgery of the Shoulder.

Thompson RC Jr, Schneider W, Kennedy T (1982), Entrapament neuropathy of the inferior branch of the suprascapular nerve by ganglia, *Clin Orthop* **166**: 185–7.

Tibone JE, Elrod B, Jobe FW et al (1986), Surgical treatment of tears of the rotator cuff in athletes, *J Bone Joint Surg (Am)* **68**: 887–91.

Torg JS (1990), Cervical spine stenosis with cord neuropathy and transient quadriplegia, *Athletic Training* **25**: 138–45.

Townsend H, Jobe FW, Pink M et al (1991), Electromyographic analysis of the glenohumeral muscles during a baseball rehabilitation program, *Am J Sports Med* **19**: 264–72.

Travlos J, Goldberg MI, Boome RS (1990), Brachial plexus lesions associated with dislocated shoulders, *J Bone Joint Surg (Br)* **72**: 68–71.

Tsairis P, Dyck PJ, Mulder DW et al (1972), Natural history of brachial plexus neuropathy. Report on 99 patients, *Arch Neurol* **27**: 109–17.

Tsairis L, Wredmark J, Johannson C et al (1991), Shoulder function in patients with unoperated anterior shoulder instability, *Am J Sports Med* **19**: 469–73.

Tullos H, King JW (1972), Unusual lesions of the pitching arm, *Clin Orthop* **88**: 169.

Turkel SF, Panio MW, Marshall JL (1981), Stabilizing mechanisms preventing anterior dislocation of the glenohumeral joint, *J Bone Joint Surg (Am)* **63**: 1208.

Uhthoff HK, Sarkar K (1991), Surgical repair of rotator cuff ruptures, *J Bone Joint Surg (Br)* **73**: 339–401.

Upton AR, McComas AJ (1973), The double crush in nerve entrapment syndrome, *Lancet* **ii**: 359.

Urist MR (1946), Complete dislocations of the acromioclavicular joint, *J Bone Joint Surg (Br)* **28**: 813.

Vogel CM, Jensen JE (1985), Effort thrombosis of the subclavian vein in a competitive swimmer, *Am J Sports Med* **13**: 269.

Waldrop JI, Norwood LA, Alvarez RG (1981), Lateral roentgenographic projection of the acromioclavicular joint, *Am J Sports Med* **9**: 337–41.

Walsh WM, Peterson DA, Shelton G et al (1985), Shoulder strength following acromioclavicular injury, *Am J Sports Med* **13**: 153–8.

Warner JJP, Micheli LJ, Arslanian LE et al (1990), Patterns of flexibility, laxity, and strength in normal shoulders and shoulders with instability and impingement, *Am J Sports Med* **18**: 366–75.

Watt I (1991), Magnetic resonance imaging in orthopaedics, *J Bone Joint Surg (Br)* **73**: 539–50.

Wong-Pack WK, Bobechko PE, Becker EJ (1980), Fractured coracoid with anterior shoulder dislocation, *J Can Assoc Radiol* **31**: 278–9.

Wood VE, Twitto R, Verska JM (1988), Thoracic outlet syndrome, *Orthop Clin North Am* **19**: 131–46.

Wright RS, Lipscomb AB (1974), Acute occlusion of the subclavian vein in an athlete: diagnosis, etiology and surgical management, *J Sports Med* **2**: 343–8.

Yoneda M, Hirooka A, Saito S et al (1991), Arthroscopic stapling for a detached superior glenoid labrum, *J Bone Joint Surg (Br)* **73**: 746–50.

Zarins B, Rowe CR (1984), Current concepts in the diagnosis and treatment of shoulder instability in athletes, *Med Sci Sports Exerc* **16**: 444.

Zilberman Z, Rejovitsky R (1982), Fracture of the coracoid process of the scapula, *Injury* **13**: 203–6.

Zuckerman JD, LeBlanc JM, Choueka J et al (1991), The effect of arm position and capsular release on rotator cuff repair, *J Bone Joint Surg (Br)* **73**: 402–5.

Index

References to Figures are in *italic*.